50 NIFTY™ SUPER

Crafts to Make with Things Around the House

By Cambria Cohen
Additional material written by Francesca Rusackas

Illustrated by Neal Yamamoto

LOWELL HOUSE JUVENILE

LOS ANGELES

NTC/Contemporary Publishing Group

NOTE: The number coming out of the paint tube in the upper right-hand corner of each craft indicates the level of difficulty, with 1 as the easiest and 3 as the hardest.

Published by Lowell House
A division of NTC/Contemporary Publishing Group, Inc.
4255 West Touhy Avenue, Lincolnwood (Chicago), Illinois 60646-1975 U.S.A.

Managing Director and Publisher: Jack Artenstein
Director of Publishing Services: Rena Copperman
Editorial Director: Brenda Pope-Ostrow
Director of Juvenile Development: Amy Downing
Editor: Joanna Siebert
Designer: Treesha Runnells
Cover Photo: Ann Bogart

Printed and bound in the United States of America

Library of Congress Catalog Card Number: 98-75608

ISBN: 0-7373-0157-0

10 9 8 7 6 5 4 3 2 1

Contents

Introduction 5

Before You Begin 6

Be Safe! 7

Creating a Craft Container .8

Make It Different! 10

  1. Magical Sand Art 11

  2. Home, Sweet Home 12

  3. Works Like a Charm! 13

  4. Sublime Chimes 14

  5. Zoetrope 16

  6. Burning the Midnight Oil 18

  7. It's a Piñata! 19

  8. Marvelous Marbleized Stationery 20

  9. Become a Master Caster! 22

10. Playing It Safe 25

11. Up, Periscope! 26

12. Getting Antsy! 27

13. The World "Accordion" to You 28

14. Cool Crayon Art 30

15. Rolling Coasters 31

16. Using Your Noodle 32

17. Eggs-ceptional! 33

18. Candle, Candle, Burning Bright 34

19. Which Witch? 36

20. Magic Mosaic 38

21. Newspaper Hammock .39

22. Fan-tastic! 40

23. Terrific Totems 42

24. You Scratch My Back 43

25. Bag It! 44

26. Lights, Camera 45

27. Shake It Up! 46

28. Carton Critters 47

29. Paper Perfect 48

30. This One's for the Birds! 50

31. What a Relief! 52

32. Soapy Sculptures 53

33. An Egg-citing Mobile 54

34. Melted Plastic Ornaments 55

35. Balloon Blastoff! 56

36. Cotton Swab Art 57

37. A Really Big Shoe 58

38. A Rose Is a Rose 59

39. Rolling in Dough 60

40. Make a Good Impression 61

41. As Time Goes By 62

42. Rockin' Candy 63

43. Paper Sculpture 64

44. Magic Crystals 66

45. Bull-Roarer 67

46. I Spy Tie-Dye 68

47. Dancing Marionettes 70

48. Lionhearted! 71

49. A Dandy Desk Set 72

50. Walking on Eggshells 73

Hosting a Craft Fair 74

The Perfect Craft 78

Craft Fair Checkoff List 80

Introduction

Looking for the perfect handmade craft? Why not make it yourself? This book is filled with ideas for making crafts using easy-to-find materials. Each of the one-of-a-kind crafts in *50 Nifty Super Crafts to Make with Things Around the House* is a blast to create! You'll find lots of tips for making each craft really special.

Before you start making any of the crafts, check out "Creating a Craft Container" on page 8. Decorating your craft container can be as much fun as doing one of the crafts! The craft container is a convenient way to store your craft supplies.

There are many crafts to choose from, so take your time as you leaf through the book. Keep in mind what items you have in your craft container, and look around your house for other materials you'll need.

If you can't find some of the craft supplies, check out "Make It Different!" on page 10. This section will give you tips for adapting some of the crafts using materials you have on hand.

If you are feeling really adventurous, think about hosting a craft fair. You can raise money for a worthy cause and have tons of fun doing it! See "Hosting a Craft Fair" on page 74 for more information.

Now, get set to create!

Before You Begin

Read the following guidelines before you start doing the crafts in this book.

Some of these crafts require help or supervision from a parent or another adult. Be sure an adult is available to help if you choose a craft marked "Adult Supervision Recommended" or "Adult Supervision Required."

Think about the level of difficulty for each craft. The number in the upper right-hand corner indicates how difficult each craft is—1 is the easiest and 3 is the hardest.

Before you begin, make sure you have enough time to complete the craft you are doing. There's nothing worse than being rushed! Also, allow enough time for a thorough cleanup.

Find a good place to make the craft, especially if it might be messy. Avoid carpeted areas, and put down newspaper or cardboard when working on a table. Some projects should be done in the garage or outside. Try to find a spot where you will not disturb others.

Keep a trash container and some paper towels close at hand in case you spill.

Wear old clothing when you make crafts that might be messy.

Read all the directions carefully before you begin a craft. Gather all the supplies you will need ahead of time. Be sure you have permission to take items if they do not belong to you.

Be Safe!

Work in a well-ventilated area or wear a mask when you are using chemicals such as spray shellac, ammonia, or bleach. Call an adult immediately if you spill chemicals on your skin or clothing, or if you inhale these chemicals.

Don't pour chemicals down the sink drain. Ask an adult to find out about your city's environmental guidelines, then follow them.

Throw leftover plaster in the trash. Never throw it down the drain, as it can clog the sink.

Wash your hands after you do each craft. Also, carefully clean your work area.

Wear protective eyewear when doing a craft that requires you to chip away at plaster.

Be sure an adult is available to help if you choose to do one of the following crafts for which adult supervision is recommended or required:

Burning the Midnight Oil (page 18)

Become a Master Caster! (page 22)

Cool Crayon Art (page 30)

Rolling Coasters (page 31)

Candle, Candle, Burning Bright (page 34)

Paper Perfect (page 48)

What a Relief! (page 52)

Soapy Sculptures (page 53)

Melted Plastic Ornaments (page 55)

Rolling in Dough (page 60)

Rockin' Candy (page 63)

Paper Sculpture (page 64)

Bull-Roarer (page 67)

I Spy Tie-Dye (page 68)

Creating a Craft Container

Putting together a craft container can be lots of fun! It's also a great way to keep your supplies together, so you can grab them when you need them.

Find a box that has a lid. You can use a shoe box or another cardboard box that is a little larger. You will be able to fit more in a larger box, but don't choose one that's too big to fit in a convenient place.

Now personalize your container. Use your imagination! You can use stickers, markers, paint, and glitter to decorate it. You can create a fun collage look with some glue, wrapping paper scraps, candy wrappers, fabric scraps, magazine cutouts, post-cards, and old stamps. When you're done, let your container dry.

Once your container is ready, you can begin to fill it with supplies. Look around the house for these basic items, but be sure to get permission before you take anything that is not yours:

- cardboard pieces
- colored markers
- colored paper
- cotton swabs
- craft glue
- craft knife (to be used with adult supervision only)
- masking tape
- needle and thread
- newspaper
- paintbrushes
- paints
- paper plates
- pencils
- plain paper
- ruler
- sandpaper
- scissors
- spray lacquer or shellac (to be used with adult supervision only)
- stapler
- tape
- toothpicks

Keep your eyes open for household items you can reuse. Add these objects to your craft container as you find them:

- aluminum foil
- broken crayons
- buttons
- egg cartons
- fabric scraps
- glass jars
- greeting cards
- juice cans
- magazines
- milk containers (clean and empty)

- nylon stockings
- plastic baskets
- plastic lids
- sequins
- stamps
- straws
- string
- wire hangers
- yarn
- yogurt containers (clean and empty)

If you have little brothers or sisters, keep your craft container someplace where they can't reach it.

Make It Different!

Don't be discouraged if you don't have all the supplies you need to create a craft. Try making the craft using materials you *do* have. Just think of other materials that would create a similar effect. The following suggestions may give you some ideas of your own.

It's a Piñata! (page 19)

If you don't have laundry starch, try making a flour paste for your papier-mâché. Mix together ½ cup flour and ⅔ cup water in a container. Stir until the paste is sort of creamy. Use a paintbrush to cover the newspaper strips with this paste, just as you would if you were using the starch mixture.

Getting Antsy! (page 27)

If you don't have an eyedropper, you can use a drinking straw to place sugar water inside the jar. Cut off part of the straw, dip it into the sugar water, place a finger over the end of the straw, and lift the straw out of the sugar water. Hold the straw over the jar, then lift your finger off the end a few times. The sugar water will drip out of the straw and into the jar.

A Rose Is a Rose (page 59)

If you don't have any colored tissue paper, you can paint coffee filters with watercolors to create a similar look. Let the coffee filters dry completely before you start creating your flower crafts.

Walking on Eggshells (page 73)

If you don't have any eggs, try using dry pasta noodles. Wide, flat pasta works best, so crush up some lasagna noodles and get ready to paint!

What other ways can you adapt some of the crafts?

Magical Sand Art

The main ingredient in this fun craft is something the world will never run out of—sand! If you don't live near a beach, collect sand from a nearby playground or park.

What You'll Need

- 9 empty glass jars or glass bottles (with lids or caps)
- powder paints, various colors
- funnel (optional)
- sand, enough to fill the jars

Directions

1. Start by filling eight of the jars half full with sand.

2. Pick a color of powder paint and pour some of it into one of the jars. Cover the jar tightly and shake it well. The paint will color the sand.

3. Repeat Step 2 with a different color of paint and a different jar of sand. Do the same with the remaining jars, putting one color of paint in each.

4. Now get the empty jar, which can be larger than the other jars. Pick one color of sand and pour it into the empty jar to create a 1" layer. (Use the funnel if you are pouring into a bottle.)

5. Choose a different color and pour another layer on top of the previous one, creating a ½" layer. Continue with the remaining colors of sand, varying the thickness of each layer. When the jar is full, put the lid on tightly. You've got a beautiful sand "sculpture."

Home, Sweet Home

Let your imagination go wild as you build your own custom-made home!

What You'll Need

- 2 boxes of sugar cubes
- construction paper, various colors
- 12" x 12" piece of cardboard
- 10" x 10" piece of cardboard
- cellophane (or plastic wrap)
- colored paper napkins
- newspaper
- glue or rubber cement
- scissors
- thread
- tape
- sandpaper

Directions

1. First, lay down some newspaper and put the larger piece of cardboard on it. Form a rectangle out of sugar cubes in the middle of the cardboard. The rectangle should be 10 cubes long and about six cubes wide. Glue the cubes together. Now glue on a second row, then a third, building upward. Leave an open rectangle for the front door by omitting two cubes from a few rows. To make windows, just omit one or two cubes from two consecutive rows to make an open square.

2. Stop when the house is six rows high. Now add the finishing touches! To cover the windows, cut out a square of cellophane and tape it over the windows from the *inside* of the house. Cut curtains out of paper napkins. Glue them to the inside of the windows and tie them back with thread.

3. Cut a roof out of the smaller piece of cardboard and fold it in half to make an upside-down "V." Set the roof over the house and glue it in place.

4. Finally, cut a straight or curved walkway out of sandpaper and glue it down so that it leads to the front door, which you can make out of construction paper. "Landscape" your house by cutting green construction paper for the lawn, trees, and bushes!

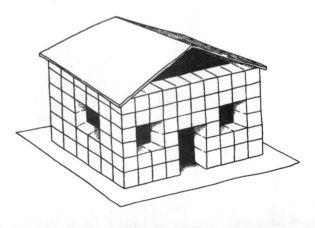

3

Works Like a Charm!

With just a few charms and simple trinkets, you can make a personal gift for your best friend or a member of your family!

What You'll Need

- small personal objects such as hair clips, buttons, perfume bottles, beads, plastic figures, erasers, rubber animals
- Popsicle® sticks (available at craft stores)
- photograph
- plastic, silver, or gold charms
- glue
- newspaper

Directions

1. To make the frame, glue 16 Popsicle sticks, edge to edge, into a flat square shape, four on each side. Overlap and glue the inner four sticks at each corner (A). Then turn the frame over and glue Popsicle sticks flat, edge to edge, to create a solid back (B).

2. Now make it charming! Lay the frame on a sheet of newspaper. Glue a charm or object onto the frame. Pick another object and glue it next to the first one.

3. Continue gluing objects. Work on alternate sides of the frame so that one side can dry while you're working on another one. Cover as much of the frame as possible.

4. Let the frame dry completely. Next, insert a photograph of the person who will receive the frame! Trim the photo if necessary, then slide it in from the side.

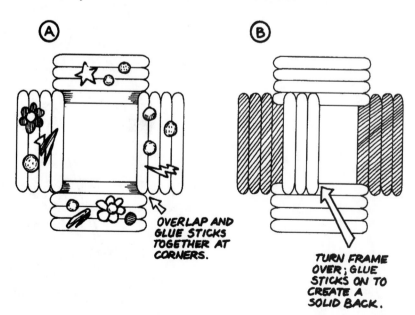

Ⓐ Ⓑ

OVERLAP AND GLUE STICKS TOGETHER AT CORNERS.

TURN FRAME OVER; GLUE STICKS ON TO CREATE A SOLID BACK.

4 Sublime Chimes

Making beautiful music is a "breeze" with these cool wind chimes!

What You'll Need

- 2 pieces of heavy cardboard, at least 16" x 6" large
- several sheets of light cardboard
- 2 or 3 metal lids
- 3 or 4 50¢ coins
- scissors
- string
- old silverware
- tape
- ruler
- large nails
- old keys
- pencil
- glue

Directions

1. Start by making a holder for your chimes. Cut two triangles out of the heavy cardboard. The base of the triangles should be 16", and the height about 6".

2. Find the midpoint at the bottom of the first triangle and cut a 3" vertical slot. Then, from the top point of the second triangle, cut a 3" vertical slot.

3. Now use the scissors to punch a row of holes, about 1" apart, across the bottom of each triangle. The holes should be ¼" from the bottom edge.

4. Next, take the first triangle and slide it into the slot on the second triangle (A). Glue them in place if necessary.

5. Cut several 4" x 1" strips of light cardboard, one for each hole you punched in the heavy cardboard. Use the scissors to poke a hole at both ends of each strip.

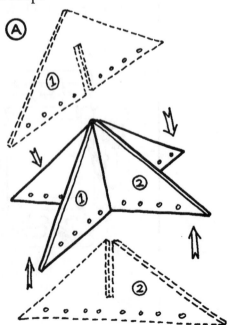

14

6. Now cut several 12" pieces of string. Tape the end of each string to a lid, coin, or piece of silverware. For the keys, thread the string through the hole and tie a knot. For the nails, tie the string around the nail under the head so it will hold.

7. Attach each chime to a strip of cardboard. Thread the free end of each piece of string through one hole and out the opposite hole in each strip (B).

8. Next, take the free end of each string again, put it through a hole in the heavy cardboard holder, and tie a big knot to secure it.

9. Poke a hole at the top of the cardboard holder. Thread a 12" piece of string through the hole and tie the ends together for hanging (B).

One Step Further

Next time you're at the beach, collect seashells to make into a pretty wind chime! Or try using small glass jars, such as baby food jars or pimiento jars, instead of metal objects.

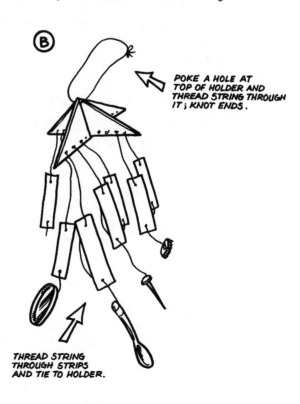

(B)

POKE A HOLE AT TOP OF HOLDER AND THREAD STRING THROUGH IT; KNOT ENDS.

THREAD STRING THROUGH STRIPS AND TIE TO HOLDER.

Zoetrope

Invented in the 1830s, the zoetrope (ZOH-uh-trohp) was an early motion-picture gadget. When it was rotated, a short movie strip came to life inside! Here's how to make a miniature version of your own.

What You'll Need

- colored pencils or markers
- black construction paper
- light cardboard
- paper cup with a flat bottom
- small bead
- scissors or craft knife
- compass
- ruler
- tape
- paper clip

Directions

1. Start by making your filmstrip. Cut a strip of cardboard 13" long and about 1½" wide. On one side of the strip, draw a moving-picture scene using the pencils or markers. You can draw a person doing cartwheels, a frog jumping, or a bird flying. When you're done, tape the ends together to form a ring, with the scene you drew on the inside of the ring.

2. To make the zoetrope, cut a strip of black construction paper 13½" long and 3" wide. Lay the strip horizontally. Place the ruler along the top edge. Starting at one end, make a mark with a pencil at $^{15}\!/_{16}$", then 1", then $1^{15}\!/_{16}$", then 2", and so on. Continue doing this all the way across the top of the strip (A).

3. Now you're going to cut slits out of the narrow areas that measure $^{1}\!/_{16}$". It might be best to use the hobby knife for this. The slits should not go farther than 1" down. Use the ruler to help you cut straight.

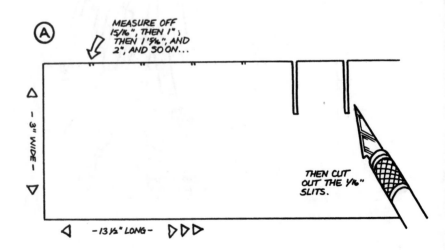

Ⓐ MEASURE OFF 15/16", THEN 1", THEN 1'9/16", AND 2", AND SO ON...

— 3" WIDE —

THEN CUT OUT THE 1/16" SLITS.

◁ — 13½" LONG — ▷▷▷

4. To create flaps across the bottom of the strip, cut a row of notches across the bottom edge. The notches should be ¼" high. Each notch should match up with each slit above (B).

5. Fold up the flaps. Tape the ends of the strip together to form a ring. Make sure the flaps are on the inside of the ring.

6. To make the base of your zoetrope, use the compass to draw a circle with a 4¼" diameter on another piece of cardboard. Cut out the circle and drop it into the ring. The circle should rest on the flaps at the bottom of the ring. Turn the zoetrope over and tape the flaps onto the base (C). Flip the zoetrope right side up again.

7. Now set the paper cup on your work surface, bottom side up. Unbend the paper clip to form a "P" shape. Poke the stem of the clip through the center of the zoetrope base. Slide the bead onto the stem and push the clip through the center of the cup (D).

8. Drop your filmstrip ring into the zoetrope ring. Position yourself so that you are eye level with the zoetrope. Use your hand to spin the ring. Look through the slits between the black squares. You'll see a moving picture! Try creating a whole bunch of filmstrips and watch them come to life in your new zoetrope!

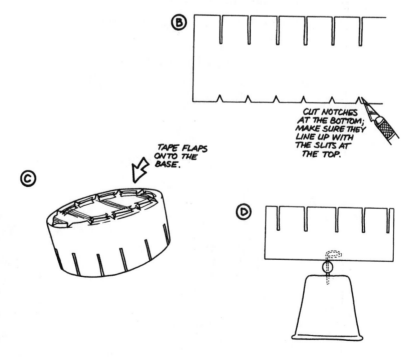

Ⓑ

CUT NOTCHES AT THE BOTTOM; MAKE SURE THEY LINE UP WITH THE SLITS AT THE TOP.

Ⓒ

TAPE FLAPS ONTO THE BASE.

Ⓓ

17

Burning the Midnight Oil

ADULT SUPERVISION REQUIRED
With just a few simple tools, you can make beautiful floating lamps that will impress your friends!

What You'll Need

- wine cork
- sharp knife
- clear, shallow bowl, wineglass, or glass jar
- tweezers (optional)
- scissors
- entire wick from an old candle
- vegetable oil
- matches
- nail
- ruler
- water

Directions

1. To begin, use the knife to cut your wine cork into slices about ⅛" thick (A).

2. Carefully poke the nail through the center of each slice. Try not to crumble the cork!

3. Next, use the scissors to cut the wick into pieces ½" long.

4. String each wick piece through the hole in each cork slice. Fray each wick at one end by pulling apart the string and flattening it against the cork (A). This will prevent the wick from coming out.

5. Keep in mind that the shape of the bowl, glass, or jar you choose will make your lamp look unique. Fill the bowl, glass, or jar half full with water.

6. Now pour enough vegetable oil on top of the water to make a ½" layer.

7. Float the cork slices on the water, frayed part of the wick down, and ask an adult to light them (B). If the glass is too deep, they can hold the match in a pair of tweezers and reach down inside the glass.

Ⓐ CUT THE CORK INTO ⅛" SLICES.

FRAY THE END OF THE WICK.

Ⓑ

It's a Piñata!

Here's a craft that's as much fun to wreck as it is to make!

What You'll Need

- large balloon
- liquid laundry starch
- tempera paint, various colors
- tissue paper, various colors
- newspaper
- paintbrush
- assorted wrapped candies
- screw ring
- cup
- string
- masking tape
- glue
- pin or needle
- water

Directions

1. Start by blowing up the balloon and tying a knot.

2. To papier-mâché the balloon, tear a few sheets of newspaper into wide strips. Mix ⅔ starch and ⅓ water in a cup. Place a strip of newspaper over the balloon. Dip the paintbrush into the starch mixture and "paint" over the strip (A). Cover the whole balloon, but leave a hole around the knot that's big enough to fit the candy in. Let the balloon dry.

3. Pop the balloon with a pin near the knot. Shake out the balloon pieces.

4. Fill the papier-mâché balloon with candy. Cover the opening with tape.

5. Now paint your piñata in bright colors. Try gluing strips of tissue paper on each end to make your piñata look like a giant piece of wrapped candy!

6. Carefully insert the screw ring into the top of the piñata. Put a string through the ring and hang the piñata from a tree in your backyard or from a basketball hoop if you have one (B).

One Step Further

Try papier-mâchéing several balloons together in the shape of an animal. Add cardboard for ears, a starched string for a tail, and strips of tissue paper for hair.

PLACE NEWSPAPER STRIPS ON BALLOON; PAINT OVER WITH STARCH MIXTURE.

Marvelous Marbleized Stationery

Once you've turned plain white paper into stunning stationery, you won't want to write on anything else!

What You'll Need

- white typing paper
- disposable baking pan (larger than the paper)
- newspaper
- white envelopes
- clean rags
- water
- pencils
- enamel oil paints (2 or 3 colors)

Directions

1. First, lay some sheets of newspaper on the table. Fill the baking pan about three-quarters full with water and place it on the newspaper.

2. Now choose an oil paint. (If you use more than three colors, your stationery will look too muddy.) Dip the pointed end of a pencil into the paint, then hold the pencil over the pan and let the paint dribble into the water (A). Repeat, using a different pencil for each color.

3. Next, "pull" the paint into different shapes by lightly running the pointed end of a clean pencil (one that doesn't have paint on it) through the water. Swirl the pencil around until you have a design you like.

4. Take a sheet of paper and carefully lay it on top of the water. Wait just a few seconds, then pick up the paper by a corner and pull it out of the water (B).

Ⓐ

5. Lay the paper, paint side up, on a clean rag and let it dry overnight. Do your writing on the white side, so the marble design is on the back.

6. No stationery set is complete without matching envelopes! You can marbleize the whole front or just the back flap. Repeat Steps 4 and 5 with a plain white envelope. If you want to marbleize only the flap, bend it up and, holding the envelope by the bottom, lay the flap on the water-and-paint mixture and pull it out.

One Step Further

Try mixing and matching colors. You can also make a marbleized journal or diary by inserting blank white sheets between two painted sheets. Make sure the painted sides face out. Punch holes in the upper and lower left-hand corners, then "bind" your diary with string or yarn.

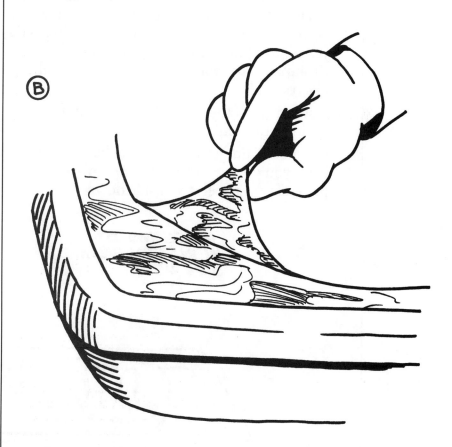

Become a Master Caster!

ADULT SUPERVISION REQUIRED

Here's how to make a perfect plaster cast of your hand. It's not as difficult as it looks!

What You'll Need

- 10-pound bag of plaster of Paris (available at hardware or paint stores)
- 2 large mixing bowls
- wooden spoon
- shallow baking pan
- petroleum jelly
- measuring cup
- wax paper
- dishwashing liquid
- water
- hammer and chisel
- pliers
- glue
- teacup
- newspaper
- paintbrush

Directions

1. First, make a mold for your cast. Lay down several sheets of newspaper to catch any plaster drippings.

2. Fill a bowl with one pint of water. Open the bag of plaster. Use the teacup to scoop out the plaster and slowly sprinkle it into the bowl of water. The plaster will start to absorb the water. Don't stir yet! Keep adding scoops of plaster until all the water is absorbed (it should take about eight teacups full) and the mixture looks like oatmeal.

3. Now stir with the spoon for three minutes. The plaster will begin to thicken.

4. Rub petroleum jelly all over the hand you're going to cast (the hand you do not write with), and place the hand on a large piece of wax paper, palm side down.

Ⓐ PLACE MOLD IN WATER, PALM SIDE UP.

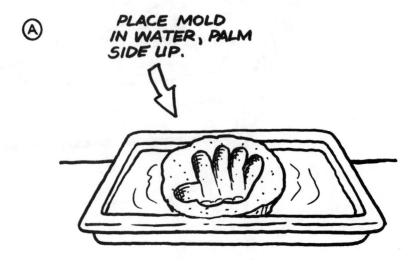

5. Have a friend or an adult use the teacup to scoop out some of the plaster mixture and pour it over your hand. Keep your hand pressed flat so no plaster gets underneath.

6. After your hand is completely covered, wait a few minutes until the plaster in the bowl thickens a bit and starts to look like sour cream. Then scoop out enough plaster to make a 1" layer on your hand. Now wait 10 more minutes while the plaster dries. Ask an adult to clean out the bowl for you before the left-over plaster dries.

7. When the plaster over your hand starts to feel warm, wiggle your fingers and slowly pull your hand out. The chunk of plaster that is left is your mold! If some of the mold breaks off when you pull out your hand, just glue the pieces back together.

8. Next, put a squirt of dishwashing liquid in another bowl and add some water to make it soapy. Then fill the shallow baking pan with water. Turn the mold over so the hand imprint is facing up. Use the paintbrush to "paint" the hand imprint with soapy water (which will make it easier to chip off the mold later). Place the mold, hand side up, in the pan of water so that only the outside of the mold gets wet (A). Hold it there for about five minutes. The outside of the mold must be completely saturated, or else it will absorb too much water out of the fresh batch of plaster that you will pour to make the cast.

9. Take out the mold and lay it on a sheet of wax paper, hand side up. Mix another batch of plaster and, when the plaster starts to get stiff, carefully pour it into the mold, filling the fingertips. Keep pouring the plaster so that it builds up to about 1" above the mold to create a base (B). Let the plaster harden; it will take at least an hour.

POUR PLASTER INTO MOLD; POUR UNTIL IT BUILDS TO 1" ABOVE THE MOLD.

Ⓑ

10. Now you need to remove the mold. You can use the pliers to break off pieces around the edge, but you'll have to use the hammer and chisel to chip away most of the mold (C). Ask an adult to help you!

11. Once the mold has been removed, soak the hand cast in some soapy water and let it dry. If you need to patch any gouges or chips, just mix a little plaster and water and fill the cracks. You've made a "hands-down" masterpiece!

One Step Further

You can shellac, varnish, or paint your plaster cast any way you want. Next time, try making a cast of your foot! Sand down the heel so that the foot stands upright with the toes pointed up. Then make another foot cast and use the two casts as bookends (or would that be foot-ends?)! Or go outside and try pouring plaster into tire tracks or animal footprints you find in the mud or dirt. When the plaster hardens, lift it up. You should get an impression of the track!

CAREFULLY CHIP AWAY MOLD.

Playing It Safe

You can turn an ordinary book into a special safe that only you know about!

What You'll Need

• old hardcover book
• rubber cement
• craft knife
• pencil
• ruler

Directions

1. First, find an old hardcover book, about 200 pages long, that no one wants. Open up the book to the first page.

2. Take the pencil and ruler and mark 1" in from all four sides of the page. Then connect the marks by drawing a rectangle.

3. Now use the ruler and the hobby knife to cut out the shape you just drew, leaving the 1" border.

4. Repeat Steps 2 and 3 with the remaining pages until the middle sections have all been cut out. Be patient—this may take awhile. Try cutting at least three or four pages at a time. When you're done, you should have a rectangle-shaped empty space inside the book!

5. Brush rubber cement along the four walls that line the empty space. This will hold the pages together. Let the rubber cement dry.

6. Now you have a place to hide your valuables! You can put money, secret messages, keys, or jewelry in the special compartment. When you close the book and put it on your bookshelf, no one will know it's a safe—except you!

BRUSH CEMENT ON INSIDE FOUR WALLS TO HOLD THE PAGES TOGETHER.

RUBBER CEMENT

Up, Periscope!

With this periscope, you'll be able to look over things and around corners!

What You'll Need

- tall, sturdy box, such as a liquor-bottle box or shoe box
- 2 small mirrors of the same size
- block of Styrofoam
- black paper or black marker
- scissors
- glue
- colored construction paper
- masking tape

Directions

1. First, cut off the top and bottom of the liquor-bottle box (if you use a shoe box, tape the lid closed before cutting). Then cut two holes at opposite ends of the box (A). The holes should be the same size as the mirrors.

2. Next, use black paper (or a black marker) to completely cover (or darken) the inside of the box. Don't cover the holes if you use black paper. Decorate the outside by gluing colored construction paper around it.

3. Cut two triangular wedges out of the Styrofoam. The wedges should fit into the corners of the box. Glue a mirror onto the widest side of each triangle (B).

4. Now glue each triangle into a corner of the box, opposite each hole you cut (C).

5. Hold the periscope vertically, look into the bottom hole, and you'll be able to see out the top!

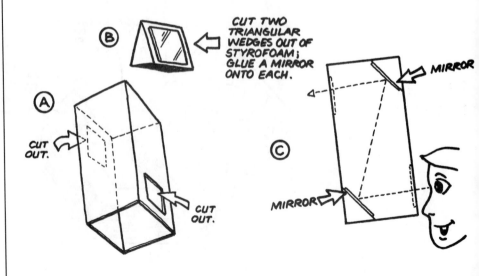

Ⓑ

CUT TWO TRIANGULAR WEDGES OUT OF STYROFOAM; GLUE A MIRROR ONTO EACH.

MIRROR

Ⓐ

CUT OUT.

CUT OUT.

Ⓒ

MIRROR

$\diamondsuit$12 Getting Antsy!

You don't need to send away for an ant farm—you can make your very own in just a few simple steps.

What You'll Need

- large glass jar (like a peanut butter jar) with a lid
- small glass jar (like a jelly or applesauce jar)
- any size jar (to catch ants)
- soil
- sugar
- eyedropper
- drinking glass
- wooden spoon
- sand
- water
- plastic tub
- bread crumbs or food scraps

Directions

1. It's best to do this project outside so that your parents won't have to worry about ants in the house! First, mix equal parts of soil and sand in a plastic tub.

2. Take the small jar and place it upside down inside the large jar (A).

3. Now you've got to catch some ants! Fill the third jar halfway with the soil and sand mixture. Mix a little sugar and water together in the drinking glass, then stir it into the soil and sand. Lay the jar on its side. The ants will be attracted to the sugar.

4. When enough ants have crawled into the jar, pour the ants and soil into the large jar. The mixture will surround the small jar. The narrow field of vision between the large and small jars will give you a good view of the ant tunnels (B). Add more soil and sand from the tub to fill up the jar.

5. Put the lid on the large jar tightly. You don't need to poke holes in the lid. Watch the ants build their own little colony right inside the jar! Once a week, open the jar and throw in a few bread crumbs or other food scraps. Add some drops of sugar water, too, using the eyedropper.

One Step Further

Instead of ants, why not try pillbugs, earthworms (the soil must be kept damp), or any kind of ground beetle.
Large glass jars also make great homes for caterpillars, spiders, and other creepy crawlies!

Ⓐ

Ⓑ

 # The World "Accordion" to You

It looks like a cutout of your house, but . . . presto! It opens up to reveal your family tree!

What You'll Need

- several feet of continuous feed computer paper (standard 8½" x 11" sheets)
- colored construction paper
- 2 pieces of cardboard, 10" wide and 13" tall
- markers and crayons
- glue
- scissors
- pencil

Directions

1. First, tear off a set of 10 sheets of computer paper. Do not tear off each individual sheet of paper. Now trace your family tree by asking your oldest relatives about their relatives and how they came to America or to the city you grew up in (A). Write the names of your earliest ancestors on the top sheet of computer paper. Then work your way down to the present. Make sure the bottom sheet is blank. If you don't need all 10 sheets, just tear off all but one of them.

2. Once that's done, you're ready to make the "house." Draw the shape of your house on a piece of cardboard. Use up as much of the cardboard as you can.

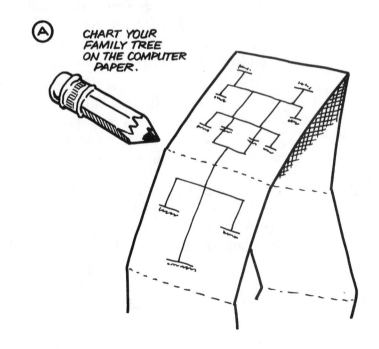

Ⓐ CHART YOUR FAMILY TREE ON THE COMPUTER PAPER.

3. Cut the shape out and put it on the second piece of cardboard. Trace around the shape, then cut the second piece of cardboard out. The two pieces will be the front and back of your house.

4. Decorate the front of your house using the colored construction paper, markers, and crayons.

5. Now decorate the back of your house, but make sure you work on the correct side, because when both decorated sides are facing outward, the shapes should mirror each other (B). When you're done, lay the back of the house colored side down, and place the front of the house over it, colored side up.

6. Take the computer paper with your family history and put it stacked between the front and back of your house. Glue the blank side of the top sheet to the inside of the front of your house. Then glue the blank bottom sheet to the inside of the back of your house. Let the glue dry overnight. When you pull the front and back sides of the house away from each other, it should open up like an accordion (C)!

Ⓑ THE DECORATED BOARDS SHOULD MIRROR EACH OTHER.

Ⓒ

Cool Crayon Art

ADULT SUPERVISION REQUIRED
Turn ordinary crayons into a beautiful wall hanging that looks like stained glass.

What You'll Need

- crayons, assorted colors
- wax paper
- scissors
- grater or pencil sharpener
- cardboard
- old pillowcase
- iron
- string
- glue
- hole punch

Directions

1. Tear off a large sheet of wax paper (about 2½' long) and lay it flat.

2. Next, make piles of crayon shavings using the grater or pencil sharpener. Spread the shavings all over the wax paper, distributing colors in whatever patterns you like. Don't put shavings near the edges.

3. Place another sheet of wax paper (the same size as the first one) over the shavings. Cover with an old pillowcase to protect the wax paper (A).

4. Now iron over the entire area of the paper. Ask an adult to help you.

5. To make the borders for your wall hanging, cut two cardboard strips. Each should be as long as the wax paper and about 2" wide. Fold the strips in half the long way.

6. Place one cardboard strip over the top end of your wall hanging so that the flaps hang over each side of the wax paper. Glue each flap down. Then glue the second strip onto the bottom of the wall hanging (B).

7. Finally, punch a hole in the top border and put a string through it. Hang your art near a window so the light can shine through!

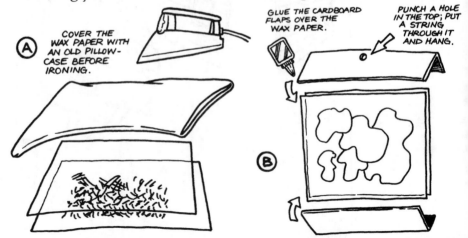

(A) COVER THE WAX PAPER WITH AN OLD PILLOW-CASE BEFORE IRONING.

GLUE THE CARDBOARD FLAPS OVER THE WAX PAPER.

PUNCH A HOLE IN THE TOP; PUT A STRING THROUGH IT AND HANG.

(B)

Rolling Coasters

ADULT SUPERVISION RECOMMENDED

In just a few simple steps, you can make the coolest coasters this side of an amusement park!

What You'll Need

- lids from margarine, cottage cheese, or yogurt containers
- old greeting cards
- glue
- scissors
- pencil
- spray shellac

Directions

1. If you'd like to make a set of coasters, they should all be the same size. Start by putting a lid on top of a greeting card illustration and tracing the lid shape onto the card. Make sure you get a portion of the illustration that will look good on your coaster! Pick the prettiest or funniest part of the card.

2. Cut out the circle. Glue the circle onto the top side of the lid. Repeat with as many lids as you like. Let them dry.

3. Take the lids outside and spray them with three coats of shellac. This will make your coasters waterproof in case any drinks spill on them. Make different sets of coasters to give as gifts!

One Step Further

What else can you use besides greeting cards? How about old photos, comics, colorful magazine ads, old wallpaper, scraps of fabric, cutup book jackets, or wrapping paper? Try natural items, too, such as whole herbs or dried leaves from your backyard. You can cut or break them to fit onto the lids. As long as you shellac the coasters, they'll be protected!

TRACE LID ON CARD AND CUT OUT.

GLUE CIRCLE ON TOP OF LID.

Using Your Noodle

Here's a nifty way to "pasta" time—making cool, colorful jewelry out of all those great macaroni and pasta shapes!

What You'll Need

- assortment of dried pasta with holes, such as macaroni, wagon wheels, penne, mostaccioli, and rigatoni
- string or heavy thread
- craft paints, various colors
- scissors
- paintbrush

Directions

1. First, gather an assortment of different pasta shapes. Before you start stringing, figure out how long you'd like your piece of jewelry to be by measuring the string around your neck, wrist, ankle, and so forth.

2. Now start threading the pasta shapes in any order you like. When you're done, tie the two ends of the string into a big knot. Cut off the excess string.

3. Try it again, only this time use craft paints to paint the pasta different colors before you string them! Give this jewelry as gifts to your friends and family.

One Step Further

Mix in other colorful objects with the pasta shapes, such as buttons and various sizes of beads, both plastic and glass. These add nice variety to your pasta jewelry. Make "drops" on a necklace by stringing two or three shapes on a short piece of string and then tying it to the necklace so that it hangs down.

Eggs-ceptional!

These little egg people are so much fun to make, you'll want to create your own eggs-clusive population!

What You'll Need

- eggs
- colored construction paper
- scissors
- lace or doilies
- yarn
- fabric scraps
- any small decorative items, such as flowers, bows, and sequins
- bowl
- tape
- glue
- felt
- crayons or markers
- needle

Directions

1. See the "Walking on Eggshells" craft (p. 73) to find out how to blow out the insides of the eggs.

2. Now give your egg people character! Cut out felt or construction paper to make eyes and noses. Use the crayons or markers to add details. Add mustaches, freckles, or goatees! For hair, glue on strands of colored yarn.

3. To make a hat, cut a circle out of construction paper. Turn it into a cone shape by cutting a narrow triangle out of the circle and bringing the edges together. Decorate the hat by cutting a piece of fabric to fit over the cone shape. Glue the fabric on, then glue lace over the fabric or cut a doily to fit.

4. Finally, make a stand for your egg person by cutting a strip of construction paper about 4" long and 1" high. Glue or tape the ends together to form a circle. Rest the egg on top. Put a little bow tie or flower on the stand, or color in a tie or collar!

Candle, Candle, Burning Bright

ADULT SUPERVISION REQUIRED

Light up the night (or day!) with your own colorful homemade candles. This project can get messy, so be careful when you're handling the hot wax!

What You'll Need

- 1 pound of paraffin (available at hardware stores)
- crayons, various colors, minus paper
- 3 milk or juice cartons
- string
- 3 pencils
- newspaper
- water
- 2 tin cans, one larger than the other
- scissors
- oven mitts

Directions

1. The cartons will serve as your candle molds. Start by cutting the tops off the cartons so you have three different heights. Put newspaper under the cartons to catch any wax drippings (A).

2. Cut three pieces of string, each a few inches longer than the height of each carton. These will be your wicks.

3. Next, tie a string around the middle of a pencil. Rest the pencil on top of the carton so that the string hangs down inside the center of it (B).

4. Now take the larger tin can and fill it halfway with tap water. Set the can on the stove on low heat. Ask an adult to help you with the next few steps.

5. Cut off a chunk of paraffin (about one-quarter of the whole block) and put it into the smaller can. Now set the smaller can inside the larger can of water. If water starts getting into the smaller can, pour out some of the water.

6. Immediately put a crayon, any color, into the smaller can. The crayon will melt and color the wax.

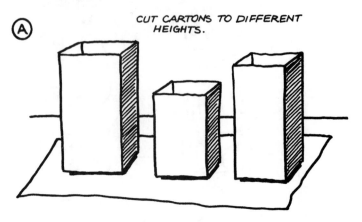

(A) CUT CARTONS TO DIFFERENT HEIGHTS.

7. Once the paraffin and crayon have melted, turn off the stove. Now put on oven mitts because the can is going to be hot! Carefully take out the smaller can and slowly pour the melted wax into one of the milk cartons (C). Stop at about 1" from the top of the carton.

8. Now be patient, because you have to let the wax cool completely. Don't move or touch the carton. When the wax has hardened, tear and peel off the milk carton. Cut the string near the pencil and remove the pencil, leaving the wick behind.

9. Repeat Steps 3 through 8 for the other cartons you have—but this time use different-colored crayons!

One Step Further

Try making a candle with different-colored layers. Follow the steps above, but use a smaller chunk of paraffin. When you pour out the melted crayon and paraffin, fill the milk carton one-third of the way. Then repeat with another small chunk of paraffin and a different-colored crayon. Continue with a variety of colors until the top layer is 1" from the top of the carton. Do red and green for a Christmas candle. Or try pink, red, and purple for a Valentine's Day gift. How about black and orange for Halloween?

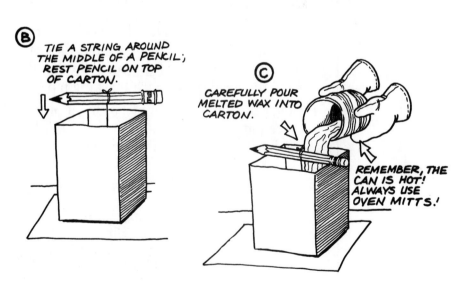

Ⓑ TIE A STRING AROUND THE MIDDLE OF A PENCIL; REST PENCIL ON TOP OF CARTON.

Ⓒ CAREFULLY POUR MELTED WAX INTO CARTON.

REMEMBER, THE CAN IS HOT! ALWAYS USE OVEN MITTS!

Which Witch?

Learn how to transform an ordinary empty bottle into a spooky witch!

What You'll Need

- empty glass bottle
- nylon stocking
- needle and thread
- orange yarn and black yarn
- cotton balls
- black tissue or crepe paper
- black construction paper
- 2 black buttons
- glue
- masking tape
- scissors
- ruler

Directions

1. To make the head, stuff a couple of handfuls of cotton balls into the foot of the stocking. Thread the needle and tie a knot at the end. You're going to make the witch's nose. Pinch the stocking between your thumb and forefinger, grabbing a wad of cotton underneath. Sew around the base of the nose, making a circle. Keep pinching the stocking and cotton while you're doing this.

2. When you're through, pull the needle and thread to tighten the stitches. The cotton will bunch up in the circle you made and stick out to form a nose. Stuff more cotton into the nose if you want. Secure your stitches by going over a previous stitch several times, making very tiny, tight stitches. Then cut off the thread.

3. Now sew on buttons for the eyes and orange yarn for the hair. Tie a knot in the stocking to hold the cotton in. Put the stocking into the mouth of the bottle so that the head rests on top. Tape the head down with masking tape.

4. Cover the witch's body by cutting a piece of black tissue or crepe paper that will fit around the bottle. Fasten the paper to the bottle with a few drops of glue.

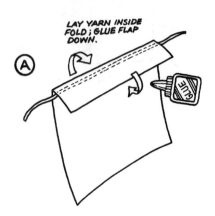

LAY YARN INSIDE FOLD; GLUE FLAP DOWN.

Ⓐ

5. To make the cloak, cut a 12" x 10" piece of black tissue or crepe paper. Lay the paper horizontally and fold the top edge down to make a 2" flap. Cut an 18" piece of black yarn and lay it inside the fold along the crease. Then glue down the flap (A). Now put the cloak around the bottle and tie the ends of the yarn together in front.

6. Don't forget the hat! Cut a 12" circle and a 4" circle out of black construction paper. Cut a narrow triangle out of the larger circle. Bring the edges together to form a cone, then glue them together. Glue the cone to the smaller circle (B).

7. Finally, add hands and feet by cutting them out of black construction paper. Glue the hands on the front of the cloak. Attach the feet to the bottom of the glass.

One Step Further

Here's another doll you can make. Peel an apple and carve out a simple face on one side. Stick the pointed end of a pencil into the bottom of the apple. Put the other end of the pencil into the mouth of a bottle so that the apple rests on top. Decorate the bottle by papier-mâchéing it and painting it. Then let the apple dry and watch it turn into the face of an old person. Be patient—it can take up to a month!

Ⓑ CUT OUT A 12" CIRCLE AND A 4" CIRCLE.

CUT A NARROW TRIANGLE OUT OF LARGER CIRCLE...

FORM A CONE...

THEN GLUE CONE TO 4" CIRCLE.

Ⓒ

Magic Mosaic

Everyday items take on a whole new meaning when you mix them in a mosaic!

What You'll Need

- large piece of cardboard, 2' square
- pencil
- toothpicks
- glue
- scissors
- string

- small, colorful, textured items such as broken eggshells, macaroni, rice, dried beans, dried peas, seashells, blades of grass, dried flowers, popcorn kernels, leaves, walnut shells, sunflower seeds, sequins, beads, cutup drinking straws

Directions

1. On the cardboard, draw a big picture using the pencil. This will be the outline for your mosaic. It can be a scene, an animal, a self-portrait—use your imagination.

2. Use dabs of glue to fasten toothpicks onto your pencil lines (A). You may need to bend or break the toothpicks for the short or curved lines.

3. Pick one item, such as sunflower seeds, and fill one section by gluing them down. Try to fill the entire space so no cardboard shows through.

4. Now choose another item, one with a different color and texture, and fill the section next to the one you just filled.

5. Repeat until all the sections are covered. It should look like a patchwork quilt! Let your mosaic dry overnight, then shake it gently to get rid of any loose pieces.

6. Use scissors to punch a hole in the two upper corners of the cardboard. Thread a 2½' piece of string through one hole, across the back of the mosaic, and out the other hole. Bring the two ends together and tie a knot at the top. Now your mosaic is ready to hang (B)!

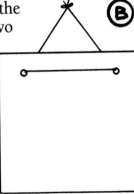

GLUE TOOTHPICKS ONTO PENCIL OUTLINES; THEN FILL SECTIONS WITH RICE, MACARONI, OR BEANS.

 # Newspaper Hammock

Instead of throwing out old newspapers, why not turn them into a hammock? Here's how.

What You'll Need

- lots of newspapers
- rope or strong clothesline
- tape
- scissors
- an old bedsheet

Directions

1. Make a stack of 30 sheets of newspaper. Roll up the stack the long way to form a tight, narrow tube. Tape the tube closed.

2. Repeat step 1 until you have about 20 tubes.

3. Cut three lengths of rope or clothesline, each at least 12' long. Lay the ropes parallel to one another.

4. Now tie each tube, one by one, to the ropes. Tie over-and-under knots, leaving 2" to 3" between each tube (A). Remember to leave at least 3' at the end of each rope so you can hang up the hammock.

5. When the hammock is long enough for you to lie in, tie the ropes together at each end (B). Hang your hammock between two trees in your backyard, or ask your mom or dad to help you hang it from your patio roof! Throw an old bedsheet over the hammock so you won't get newsprint on your clothes.

One Step Further

Try making a hammock out of brown paper shopping bags. Cut the bottom off each, then cut along a side seam and spread open the bag. Stack several bags, then roll them up.

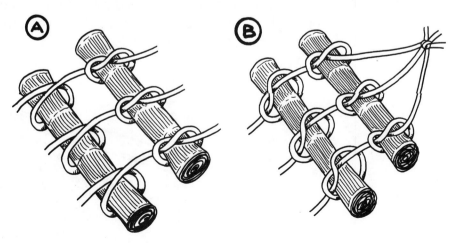

 **Fan-tastic!**

This handmade fan is perfect for a hot summer day!

What You'll Need

- about 20 Popsicle® sticks (available at craft stores)
- light cardboard
- crayons, markers, or tempera paints, various colors
- masking tape
- scissors
- glue

Directions

1. First, cut the cardboard to make the front and back pieces of your fan. They should be the same size and shape, and the shape can be anything you want. The fan should be about 9" wide. Cut a semicircle out of the bottom of each piece.

2. Draw a design on one side of the front piece. Do the same with the back piece.

3. To make the "ribs," lay a Popsicle stick flat and put some glue on one end. Then lay the end of another Popsicle stick over the glue and press the sticks together (A). You've made one rib. Repeat until you have three ribs.

4. Lay the front piece of your fan flat, colored side down. Glue the ribs onto the plain side, bringing the three ends together to form a point as shown. Then glue one Popsicle stick to each corner, bringing their ends to a point as well (B). Let the glue dry.

5. Pick up the back piece of the fan and glue it onto the front piece, matching up the edges. The two plain sides should be facing each other. Let the glue dry.

6. Next, make the handle by laying five Popsicle sticks flat. Put a piece of masking tape across the top and the bottom. This is one half of your handle. Repeat using five more sticks and two more strips of tape.

GLUE STICKS TOGETHER TO MAKE "RIB."

7. Take one half of the handle and turn it over so that the tape is on the bottom. Now glue the ends of the fan ribs onto the handle.

8. Take a single Popsicle stick and break off a 2" piece. Glue this piece across the bottom of the handle half (C). Let dry.

9. Now take the other half of the handle and glue it, masking-tape side up, onto the first half (C). The fan ribs should be sandwiched between the two halves.

10. When the glue dries, wrap masking tape around the handle from top to bottom. Color the handle using crayons, markers, or paint.

One Step Further

You can decorate your fan in various fun ways. Try gluing on lace, sequins, glitter, feathers, old jewelry, fabric scraps, pieces of pretty gift wrap . . . use your imagination! You can also make a longer handle by gluing sticks end to end, like you did to make the ribs.

BREAK OFF A 2" PIECE AND GLUE ACROSS THE HANDLE...

THEN GLUE HANDLE HALVES TOGETHER.

Terrific Totems

You only need a few items to make these colorful totem poles!

What You'll Need

- empty toilet paper tubes
- crayons or markers
- colored construction paper (light colors work best)
- glue
- scissors

Directions

1. To start, cut a piece of construction paper large enough to wrap around a toilet paper tube.
2. Lay the paper flat and use the crayons or markers to draw a colorful totem face. Remember to start drawing the face in the middle of the paper. Leave space for the three-dimensional nose.
3. When you're done, wrap your totem face around the paper tube and secure it in the back with glue.
4. Now cut a nose out of construction paper. You can color the nose or just keep it the color of the construction paper. Make a crease down the middle of the nose and glue the edges onto your totem pole as shown. Pinch the nose along the crease to make it stick out.
5. Finally, cut a pair of wings out of construction paper and color them. Be sure to make the inner edge of each wing flat. Now glue the wings onto the totem pole. Make a whole set of funny or scary totems!

One Step Further

Try stacking your totem poles one on top of the other for a different effect. You can also use paper towel tubes instead of toilet paper tubes for bigger totems!

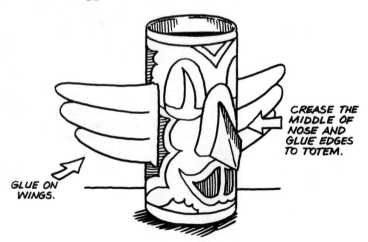

CREASE THE MIDDLE OF NOSE AND GLUE EDGES TO TOTEM.

GLUE ON WINGS.

You Scratch My Back . . .

For a quick and crazy craft, try this nifty crayon scratch art.

What You'll Need

- cardboard from a dress shirt package
- crayons, various colors, including several black crayons
- sharp objects, such as a paper clip, a ballpoint pen, a fork, a comb, scissors, a compass point, a safety pin, a coin, and a spoon

Directions

1. Start by drawing all over the entire surface of the cardboard using the crayons. Use as many colors as you like, but save the black crayons for later. The more colors you use, the better.

2. Now cover your crayon drawing with black crayon (A). Press hard! Again, cover the entire surface. Make sure you have enough black crayons!

3. Next, take the sharp objects and scratch a picture out of the black crayon (B). Scratch out a picture of your house, your pet, a castle—anything you like. Be sure to scratch just hard enough to take the black off without removing the colored crayon underneath. Use a variety of objects. A paper clip makes a thin line, while the edge of a spoon makes a wider line. Don't remove all the black crayon, though—it helps make the assortment of colors underneath shine through!

One Step Further

Here's a similar art project using black watercolor paint. Draw a picture on a piece of white paper and color it with crayons, but leave some white areas showing. Then lightly paint black watercolor over the picture. The crayon marks will "resist" the watercolor, and the paint will stay on the white areas of the paper, giving you a nice mix of paint and crayon.

Bag It!

Here's how to turn an old pair of blue jeans into a cool-looking purse, gym bag, or beach bag!

What You'll Need

- an old pair of blue jeans
- needle and thread
- heavy scissors

Directions

1. Start by cutting off the legs of the jeans about an inch below the fly. Save the legs to make into a strap.

2. If you've never sewn before, ask a parent or older brother or sister to help you out. It's very easy. Cut a long piece of thread about the length of your arms outspread. Then thread it through the needle and tie the ends together in a knot.

3. Bring together the front and back of the jeans at the bottom and sew it closed (A). Make small, tight stitches. You should go back and forth over your stitches at least twice to reinforce the bottom.

4. Next, you'll need to make a clasp to hold the top of the bag closed. Cut off the front button above the fly. Move the button to the back waistline and sew the button on the inside as shown (B). Now, to close the bag, just push the newly sewn button through the original buttonhole!

5. To make the strap, fold one of the pants legs in half the long way and sew it closed.

6. Now sew each end of the strap to the inside of the waistline (C). Sew the strap securely, otherwise it may break when your bag is full. Now you're a real blue-jean baby!

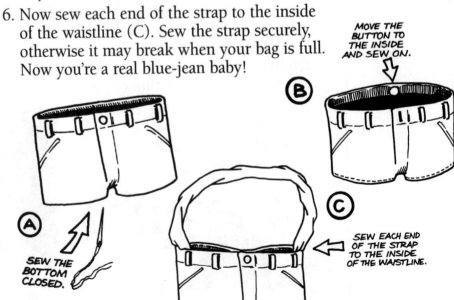

MOVE THE BUTTON TO THE INSIDE AND SEW ON.

(A) SEW THE BOTTOM CLOSED.

(B)

(C) SEW EACH END OF THE STRAP TO THE INSIDE OF THE WAISTLINE.

26 Lights, Camera . . .

Follow these simple steps to become an amateur film projectionist!

What You'll Need

- clear acetate (available at art-supply stores)
- half-gallon milk carton
- markers, various colors
- scissors
- flashlight
- tape
- ruler

Directions

1. Begin by washing and drying the milk carton thoroughly. Cut off the top and the bottom so that you have a rectangular tube for your "viewer."

2. Next, cut two slits, each about 3" high, on opposite sides of the carton (A).

3. Now cut strips of acetate, each just under 3" wide. Tape them together into one long "filmstrip."

4. Use a marker to divide the acetate strip into a series of frames, each about 3½" wide. Now, leaving the first frame empty, draw scenes on the frames using different-colored markers. The scenes should tell a story.

5. Slide your "filmstrip" through one slit in the carton and out the other so that the first scene is inside the carton.

6. Turn off the lights. Shine the flashlight through an open end of the carton and onto a blank wall (B). The images you drew will be projected onto the wall. Pull the acetate through, frame by frame, until your "movie" is over!

One Step Further

Add color and character to your film projector by covering it with construction paper. Or papier-mâché it and then paint it. Add the name of your favorite movie theater. Make miniature projectors with pint-size cartons or quart-size cartons.

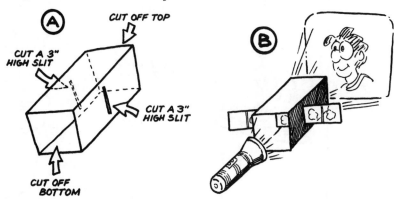

(A) CUT OFF TOP
CUT A 3" HIGH SLIT
CUT A 3" HIGH SLIT
CUT OFF BOTTOM

(B)

Shake It Up!

In just a snap, you can make a snazzy snow-dome paperweight like those you see in souvenir shops!

What You'll Need

- empty baby food jar with lid
- small amount of rubber cement
- small plastic flower and stem
- teaspoon
- silver glitter
- water
- glue

Directions

1. First, clean out the baby food jar. Wash the label off.

2. Hold the flower next to the jar. If it's taller than the jar, cut the stem to fit.

3. Next, take the lid and turn it upside down so that the inside part is facing up. Put the lid on the table and put a drop or two of rubber cement in the center of the lid.

4. Attach the flower by sticking its stem in the rubber cement (A). Hold the flower for a few minutes until the rubber cement hardens. If the flower is not secure, add another drop or two of rubber cement and let it dry.

5. Now fill the jar with water until the water is about ¼" from the top. Put 2 teaspoons of the glitter into the water for the "snow."

6. Put glue around the inside edge of the lid, and put a few drops of glue around the rim of the jar, too (B). Screw the lid on. Make sure the jar is upright (the flower will be hanging upside down), and let the glue dry.

7. Turn the jar so the flower is upright. Shake, shake, shake!

One Step Further

Substitute small plastic figures for the plastic flower. Make sure they fit in the jar, though. Put in sequins instead of glitter, or combine the two! Use a jelly jar or other glass jar— then you can use larger plastic figures and add twice as much "snow"!

(A) CEMENT FLOWER TO CENTER OF LID.

APPLY GLUE TO INSIDE OF LID...

...AND TO THE JAR'S RIM.

(B)

Carton Critters

The steps below will show you how to make a chick out of an egg carton, but after that, think of some critters to make on your own!

What You'll Need

- cardboard egg carton
- tempera paints, various colors
- buttons, feathers, sequins, colored tissue paper
- paintbrush
- scissors
- glue
- ruler

Directions

1. To make the head, cut off an end pair of cones from the egg carton. On one side of each cone you will see a pointed piece. This is the chick's beak. Hold on to this piece and trim off about ¾" around the edge of the cone. Don't cut off the beak!

2. Fold out the beak on each cone so that it sticks out. Put glue around the edge of one cone. Turn the other cone upside down and press it down on top of the first cone, matching up the beak pieces (A). Let the glue dry, then trim the beak a little.

3. Now it's time to make the chick's body. Cut off another pair of cones (not the other end pair). Each of these cones will have two points sticking up. Hold on to the points of one cone and trim off about ¾" around the edge (don't cut off the points—they're your chick's wings). Take the other cone and do the same, but this time cut off its two points.

4. Fold out the two points on the first cone to make them stick out. Then take the second cone and glue it on top of the other cone (B).

5. Now glue the head onto the body. Let it dry.

6. Paint the chick yellow with an orange beak. Glue on buttons for eyes and feathers for its tail. Add sequins and pieces of tissue paper to make it bright and cheerful!

Ⓐ

MATCH UP THE "BEAKS" AND GLUE TOGETHER.

Ⓑ

Ⓒ

Paper Perfect

Did you know that you can actually make a sheet of paper right in your own home? Here's how!

What You'll Need

- 30 sheets of regular facial tissue
- baking pan, baking dish, or tub (about 8" x 10" large and 2" deep)
- iron
- large mixing bowl
- liquid measuring cup
- piece of wire window screen, small enough to fit in the pan, dish, or tub
- eggbeater
- liquid laundry starch
- newspaper
- clean rag
- hot water

Directions

1. Before you begin, lay down at least a dozen sheets of newspaper. These will serve as your blotters.

2. First, you'll need to make the pulp. Fill the bowl halfway with hot water (but not too hot to touch). Shred the tissues into small pieces and put them in the water. Put your fingers in the water and shred the tissues further until they dissolve. The pulp will look like thin breakfast cereal.

3. Mix in 2 ounces of starch to help strengthen the paper.

4. Now pour the pulp into the baking pan, dish, or tub. Add enough water to raise the level to at least 1" from the bottom of the pan. Stir vigorously using the eggbeater.

5. Next, slide the screen into the water, then slowly pull it out using both hands. Some of the pulp will be carried out with the screen. Hold the screen over the pan to drain the excess water, and gently shake the screen to distribute the pulp evenly (A).

6. When almost all the water has drained off, lay the screen on the newspapers. Let the pulp dry until it is damp.

7. While the paper is still damp, peel it off the screen. Put a clean rag over the paper and press it with a warm iron (B). This will compress the fibers and strengthen the paper. You should be able to make four to six sheets of paper with each batch of your "paper recipe."

One Step Further

Substitute newspapers or typing paper for the facial tissues. Try adding a few drops of enamel oil paints for color. Take sheets of notebook paper, put them between two sheets of your homemade paper, and bind them together to make a diary or journal!

Ⓐ

GENTLY SHAKE SCREEN
TO EVENLY DISTRIBUTE
THE PULP.

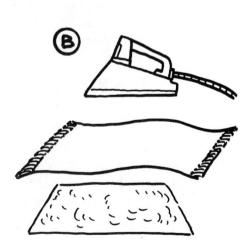

Ⓑ

This One's for the Birds!

Have fun watching your fine feathered friends by creating these simple but effective bird feeders using ordinary household objects! You can buy birdseed at any grocery or pet supply store.

Directions

Bleach Bottle Feeder

For this feeder, cut four 3" x 3" windows out of the sides of an empty, rinsed bleach bottle. The windows should start 1" from the bottom of the container. Sand down the rough edges with sandpaper or cover the edges with black electrical tape. Next, use a hammer and large nail to poke a hole in the middle of the bottle cap. Cut a 12" piece of string and tie the two ends together. Then thread the looped end through the hole and tie a big knot so the string won't slip through the hole. Now you've got a big loop to hang the bottle feeder from a tree branch or a nail in your roof.

BLEACH BOTTLE FEEDER

PLASTIC BOTTLE FEEDER

Plastic Bottle Feeder

Cut a 3" x 4" window out of an empty 2-liter plastic bottle. The window should be about 2" from the bottom of the bottle. Sand down the edges or tape over them. Now take an empty pie tin and glue it to the bottom of the plastic bottle. To hang up this bird feeder, follow the directions for the Bleach Bottle Feeder.

Mesh Bag Feeder

The mesh bag from fruit or vegetables you buy at some grocery stores makes an ideal bird feeder. You could even use a small mesh laundry bag if you can't find a fruit or vegetable bag. Just fill the empty bag half full with birdseed and tie a knot at the top of the bag. Put string through a hole at the top, tie both ends together, and it's ready to hang!

MESH BAG FEEDER

Pinecone Feeder

Pick up a pinecone or two next time you're walking through your neighborhood or a park. Mix together half a jar of peanut butter, a handful of birdseed, and a handful of uncooked oatmeal in a bowl until the mixture is gooey and sticky. With a butter knife, smear the mixture all over the pinecone. Tie a string around the top for hanging.

SPREAD PEANUT BUTTER-BIRDSEED-OATMEAL MIX ON PINECONE.

PINECONE FEEDER

Doughnut Feeder

You only need a doughnut, two jar lids, some string, and a hammer and nail to make this fun feeder! Use the hammer and nail to make a small hole in the center of each lid. Cut a 12" piece of string. Thread the string through one lid, then through the doughnut hole, then through the other lid. Tie a knot under the bottom lid. Tie the other end of the string onto a tree branch and let it hang (the lids and the doughnut will touch each other). Watch the birds flock to your new feeder!

DOUGHNUT FEEDER

One Step Further

Try making a Nest Helper. Find a pants hanger that has a cardboard tube around the bottom. With a craft knife, cut a row of slats on both sides of the tube. Stuff strands of thread or light string into the slats so that they hang down. Put the hanger on a branch and watch the birds take the thread to build their nests!

PUT STRING THROUGH SLATS.

NEST HELPER

What a Relief!

ADULT SUPERVISION REQUIRED
You can have a ball molding homemade dough into a nifty relief map—and learn a little about geography at the same time!

What You'll Need

- 3 cups flour
- 1 cup salt
- 3 tablespoons dry wheat paste powder
- 1¼ cups lukewarm water
- wooden spoon

- 11" x 17" piece of cardboard
- 11"x 17" piece of white construction paper
- large mixing bowl
- craft paints, various colors

- glue
- frying pan
- pencil
- atlas
- paintbrushes

Directions

1. Begin by drawing the shape of the United States on the white construction paper. Use an atlas as a guide. Glue the paper onto the cardboard.

2. You need to make the dough next. Heat the salt in the frying pan over low heat for about five minutes. Then mix the salt, flour, and paste powder together in a bowl. Slowly add the luke-warm water as you continue to stir. If the mixture feels too dry, add water. Knead the dough until it's soft and pliable.

3. Then, still using the atlas as a guide, use chunks of dough to fill in your map! Do the mountain ranges first, starting with the Sierra Nevadas. Make some mountaintops low and ragged, others high and smooth. Fill in the rest of the map with dough, then let it dry.

4. Now paint the details! Put snow and trees on the mountain-tops. Paint in all the lakes, rivers, and waterways. Paint each state a different color, and use a smaller brush to add the name of each state.

Soapy Sculptures

ADULT SUPERVISION REQUIRED
Learn how to turn a plain bar of soap into a "squeaky clean" sculpture!

What You'll Need

- bar of soap, any kind
- kitchen knife
- pencil

Directions

1. First, use the pencil to draw the outline of an animal directly on the bar of soap. Take up as much of the bar as you can. Draw a bear, cat, fish, alligator, bird—any animal you'd like. Refer to a photo book of real animals if you need help.

2. Take the knife and carve around the outline you drew, cutting off the excess soap.

3. Now use the knife to carefully shape the animal and make it three-dimensional. Be careful not to cut yourself. You can sprinkle water on the soap to help you mold it more easily. Water also gets rid of any mistakes you may make!

4. Cut small notches to show muscle definition. Try making cross-hatching marks to add texture. For example, if you're carving an alligator, a cross-hatching pattern on its back will make your gator look more real.

One Step Further

For variety, try different-colored soaps. Try making a lizard out of a bar of green soap. Turn a pink cake of soap into a flamingo or white soap into a swan. Or try your hand at sculpting other objects such as seashells or mushrooms. To make your soapy creations more realistic, paint them with craft paints! (If you paint them, just use them for decoration—don't wash your hands with them!)

An Egg-citing Mobile

Colored eggshells are what give this fun mobile an egg-stra special look!

What You'll Need

- 7 raw eggs
- construction paper, any color
- small paintbrushes
- craft paints, various colors
- penny
- pencil
- scissors
- needle and thread
- tissue or crepe paper, various colors
- wire hanger
- cup
- liquid laundry starch
- ruler
- water
- large mixing bowl

Directions

1. Follow the directions under "Walking on Eggshells" (p. 73) to blow out the insides of the eggs. Then cut or tear small strips of the tissue or crepe paper. Papier-mâché the eggshells and the wire hanger with bright colors (see "It's a Piñata!" on p. 19 for directions). You can also paint some of the eggshells with craft paints.

2. Using the pencil, trace the penny on the construction paper and cut it out. Cut a 16" piece of thread, double it up, and thread the needle, tying a big knot at the end of the thread.

3. Now poke the needle through the center of the construction paper circle. Slide the circle all the way down to the knot (A).

4. Choose an eggshell. Push the needle through the smaller hole. Shake the egg gently to make the needle come out the larger hole. Grab the needle and slide the eggshell down to the paper circle (A). Cut off the thread and tie it onto the bottom of the hanger so that the egg hangs down.

5. Repeat Steps 2 through 4 for the remaining eggs, except cut alternating long and short pieces of thread so the eggs hang at varying lengths (B).

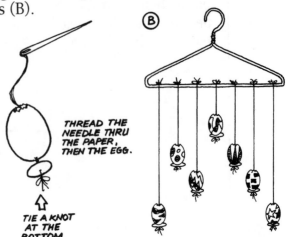

Ⓐ

THREAD THE NEEDLE THRU THE PAPER, THEN THE EGG.

TIE A KNOT AT THE BOTTOM.

Ⓑ

Melted Plastic Ornaments

ADULT SUPERVISION REQUIRED
Here's a way to make cool ornaments right in your own kitchen!

What You'll Need

- plastic berry baskets
- small glass beads
- plastic-coated wire (available at hardware stores)
- 3- or 4-quart saucepan
- aluminum pie pan
- water
- kitchen tongs
- scissors
- glue
- glitter
- ruler

Directions

1. Fill the saucepan with water and heat it on the stove (but don't boil it). The water should be deep enough to completely cover the basket.

2. Drop a plastic basket into the hot water. When the basket has collapsed and changed shape, pull it out using the tongs. Put it on a pie pan to cool.

3. Now string some glass beads onto a 24" piece of coated wire. Make sure to cut off any wire ends that are showing. Weave the beads in and out of the holes in the basket. The wire will conform to the shape of the basket.

4. Put dabs of glue on various areas of the basket and sprinkle glitter over it.

5. To make a hanger, cut another piece of coated wire about 5" long. Weave it through one of the holes. Tie both ends together at the top.

One Step Further

Try dropping a plastic cup into the hot water. It will melt into a nifty bell shape. Use colored cups for variety. To make a hole for hanging, ask an adult to heat the point of a large sewing needle by holding a lit match to it for a few seconds. Then poke a hole in the plastic with the heated needle.

TO MAKE A HANGER, WEAVE A WIRE THROUGH AND TIE A KNOT.

WEAVE THE WIRED BEADS THROUGH THE BASKET.

Balloon Blastoff!

Learn how to make a nifty balloon rocket that actually takes off! You'll need a friend to help you with this one.

What You'll Need

- fishing line
- balloon
- masking tape
- plastic drinking straw

Directions

1. Start by measuring out a piece of fishing line the length of your bedroom or living room.
2. Tie one end to a doorknob or a piece of heavy furniture at one end of the room.
3. Next, run the fishing line through a straw. Then stretch the line across the room and attach the other end to another doorknob or piece of furniture.
4. Blow up the balloon and pinch the end to hold in the air. Have your friend tape the top of the balloon to the straw so that the balloon hangs down.
5. Still holding the balloon closed, walk the straw and balloon to one end of the fishing line. Turn so that you are facing the opposite end of the fishing line.
6. Now start your countdown! When you reach zero, let go of the balloon. The escaping air will act as jet propulsion to push the balloon forward on the fishing line!

One Step Further

You can string more than one fishing line across the room and have a balloon-rocket race with your friends. Or you can use this method as an intercom to send secret messages to your brother or sister in another room. Just tape a note to the balloon and let 'er rip! Experiment a little. Get an adult to help you string fishing line from the roof or a tree so your blastoff can be vertical!

36 Cotton Swab Art

Create a nifty double-sided piece of art using simple cotton swabs!

What You'll Need

- 3 to 4 large boxes of cotton swabs (those with wooden sticks work best)
- color markers
- craft paints, various colors
- narrow paintbrush
- light cardboard
- scissors
- tape
- ruler
- 2 pieces of plastic canvas, about 6½" x 6½" with 5 holes per inch (available in the needlepoint section at craft stores)

Directions

1. To start, push a cotton swab through a square in one piece of the plastic canvas. You're going to fill the whole canvas using the swabs.

2. Now line up the second piece of canvas with the first one. Push the swab through the second piece to "connect" the canvases.

3. Take another swab and poke it through each canvas next to the first swab. Continue doing this, filling up each row (A). When you're through, the two pieces of canvas should stand upright on their own.

4. Now turn one side of the canvas toward you. Think of an outdoor scene, a mosaic, whatever you like. Then start painting the tips of the swabs (B). Be careful not to make a mistake (it will be difficult to replace the swabs). When you're done, paint a different scene or design on the other side.

5. To make the frame, measure the space between the two pieces of canvas. Cut a strip of cardboard so that it is a little wider than that space. The strip should be long enough to wrap all the way around your artwork.

6. Color the frame using the paints or markers. Then wrap it around your cotton swab art and tape it at the bottom (B). Your masterpiece is done!

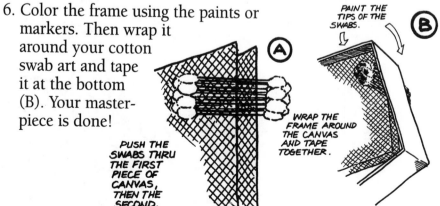

PAINT THE TIPS OF THE SWABS. (B)

WRAP THE FRAME AROUND THE CANVAS AND TAPE TOGETHER.

(A)

PUSH THE SWABS THRU THE FIRST PIECE OF CANVAS, THEN THE SECOND.

A Really Big Shoe

Take a "step" in the right direction by turning an old shoe into a playful planter!

What You'll Need

- big, old shoe (canvas works best, but leather is fine, too)
- small indoor or outdoor plant (such as a cactus or African violet) that fits inside the shoe
- liquid laundry starch
- newspaper
- paintbrush
- tempera paints, various colors
- water
- cup

Directions

1. Before you begin, lay some sheets of newspaper on your work table.

2. Now put the shoe on the newspaper. If there are any shoelaces, remove them. Papier-mâché the entire shoe, following the instructions given in "It's a Pinata!" (p. 19). Do two layers of papier-mâché, allowing the first layer to dry before you apply the next.

3. Once the shoe is stiff and dry, paint it! Be creative. Make lightning bolts, symbols, or fake buckles and laces. Let the paint dry overnight.

4. Now, leaving the plant in its original pot, place it inside the shoe. Try this nifty craft again using a different kind of shoe—maybe a high-top or a penny loafer!

38 A Rose Is a Rose

Even a paper rose by any other name is still a beautiful rose.

What You'll Need

- red and green tissue paper
- cup or bowl
- scissors
- wire stems and florist's tape (available at florist's shops)
- glass bottle
- pencil
- stapler
- ruler

Directions

1. First, cut 18 squares of red tissue paper. Each square should be 4" x 4".

2. Next, put the cup or bowl upside down on a stack of about four tissues and trace around it with the pencil. Cut out the circles. Repeat until you have 18 circles.

3. Then make a small loop at one end of a wire stem. Thread six circles onto the stem by poking the pointed end through the center of each circle. Bunch the circles loosely around the loop, then staple them once at the bottom (A).

4. Do the same with six more circles and staple them onto the others. Then repeat with the last six circles.

5. Now cut a long piece of florist's tape. With one hand, hold one end of the tape over the last staple. Use your other hand to wrap tape around the bottom of the flower about three or four times. Then continue winding tape down and around the stem.

6. Don't forget the leaves! Cut four 4" x 4" squares out of the green tissue paper. Now stack them and cut out a three-leaf shape. Tape the leaves onto the wire (B).

7. Finally, fluff out the rose layer by layer so it looks like it's in bloom. You can put it into a small glass bottle that's been decorated with papier-mâché or paints and give it as a gift!

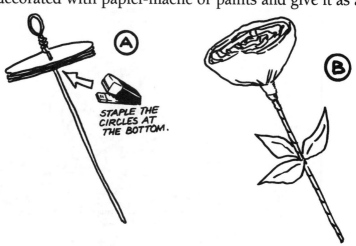

STAPLE THE CIRCLES AT THE BOTTOM.

Rolling in Dough

ADULT SUPERVISION RECOMMENDED
You'll be amazed at all the things you can do with this homemade dough. Just follow the simple recipe below.

What You'll Need

- 4 cups flour
- 1 cup salt
- 1½ cups water
- large mixing bowl
- newspaper
- nonstick (or greased) disposable cookie sheet
- craft paints, various colors
- wooden spoon
- paintbrush
- spray lacquer
- oven mitts

Directions

1. In the mixing bowl, combine the flour, salt, and water and mix well with the wooden spoon.
2. Mold the dough into different shapes, such as fruits, vegetables, animals, creepy insects, or miniature animals. Spread them out on the cookie sheet and bake at 350 degrees for one hour.
3. Use oven mitts to take out the dough and let it cool. Then paint the shapes.
4. When the paint is dry, take the figures outside and place them on sheets of newspaper. Spray them with lacquer to keep the paint from chipping.

One Step Further

You can make all sorts of crafts with this moldable dough. Glue a magnet on the back of your creation and stick it on the refrigerator. Make Christmas or Hanukkah ornaments. Just glue a piece of thread or string on the back of the ornament and it's ready to hang! You can also roll beads of different shapes, poke a nail through each to make a hole, and bake the beads. Then paint them, string them, and make necklaces and bracelets!

40 Make a Good Impression

Did you know that you can create interesting textures and patterns using simple household objects—including fruits and vegetables?

What You'll Need

- tempera paints, various colors
- apples, potatoes, starfruit
- stack of continuous feed computer paper
- several sponges
- empty spools, clothespins, buttons, corks, bottle caps
- 2 wooden dowels, at least 1" wider than the computer paper
- glue
- scissors
- string
- kitchen knife
- several empty milk cartons
- ruler

Directions

1. First, prepare your printing tools. Slice a raw potato in half and carve a heart on the inside of one half. Then dig out the potato around the heart so that the heart sticks up. Leave the other half uncut. Do the same with the apple, except cut a different shape. Cut the starfruit in half. Cut some of the sponges into squares, circles, and triangles.

2. To make a stamp pad, cut a clean milk carton to about 3" high. Cut a sponge to fit, moisten it with water, and pour some paint on it. Do the same with another milk carton and a different color of paint.

3. Spread out several sheets of computer paper, but don't tear them apart.

4. Now go stamp crazy! Choose a printing tool, such as one mentioned above, dip it in your stamp pad, and stamp it all over the paper (A). Repeat with a different tool and a different color. Be sure to leave the paper blank at the top and bottom to roll around the dowel.

5. When you're finished, tear your artwork off at the top and bottom and let it dry. Then put glue on a wooden dowel and roll the top sheet around it twice. Take the second dowel and do the same with the bottom sheet.

6. Cut a piece of string about 2' long. Tie each end to opposite ends of the top dowel. Now your artwork is ready to hang (B)!

As Time Goes By

Dig out those mementos of yours and turn them into a great gift your mom or dad will treasure forever!

What You'll Need

- large piece of cardboard, at least 16" by 20"
- crayons, markers, and paints (various colors)
- paintbrush
- scissors
- glue
- award ribbons, certificates, report cards, tests, book reports, baby photos, your horoscope, your baby bracelet, school assembly programs, pictures you drew, a lock of your hair, and other mementos

Directions

1. Make sure you have permission from an adult to use all the mementos you've chosen for this project. Gather all your mementos in front of you. Take some of the bigger items—such as newspaper clippings and pictures you drew—and trim them into different shapes.

2. Start gluing the items on the cardboard one by one. You might want to arrange them loosely in some sort of design first, then glue them down. Or just put them down in a random pattern. Overlap the items so no cardboard shows through.

3. Now add artistic flair to your collage by swashing strokes of paint here and there, outlining some of the items in crayon, and underlining important things in marker.

4. Once your collage is finished, ask an adult to help you get it framed. You can buy the supplies to make a frame at an art store, or have the art store frame the picture for you. This collage makes a wonderful gift for your mom or dad. After all, you wouldn't be here if it weren't for them!

Rockin' Candy

ADULT SUPERVISION REQUIRED

In one week, you can grow your own rock candy mountain. See if you can wait that long to eat it!

What You'll Need

- 1 cup water
- 4 cups sugar
- piece of heavy cord (the length of the jar)

- 3- or 4-quart saucepan
- large glass jar
- oven mitts
- wooden spoon

- dinner plate
- pencil

Directions

1. To begin, put the water and 2 cups of the sugar into the saucepan and heat over the stove, stirring with the wooden spoon until the sugar has dissolved.

2. Stir in the remaining 2 cups of sugar little by little. Continue heating until all the sugar has dissolved. Then have an adult help you pour all the liquid into the glass jar, using oven mitts.

3. Now tie one end of the cord around the middle of the pencil. Balance the pencil over the mouth of the jar so that the cord hangs down into the liquid. In a few hours, sugar crystals will begin to form on the cord.

4. The next day, take out the cord and place it on a dinner plate. You'll notice that crystals have also formed on the sides of the jar. To get rid of these, pour the liquid out of the jar into the saucepan and reheat it.

5. When the liquid is hot (but not boiling), have an adult help you pour it back into the jar, using oven mitts. The liquid will dissolve the crystals on the sides of the jar. Let the liquid cool.

6. When the liquid is lukewarm, put the cord with the crystals back into the jar, resting the pencil over the mouth.

7. Repeat Steps 4 through 6 every day for a week until you have a big rock candy mountain!

Paper Sculpture

ADULT SUPERVISION REQUIRED
Don't get this challenging craft confused with papier-mâché. Paper sculpture involves bending, scoring, and folding flat paper to make three-dimensional art! The steps below will show you how to make a paper-sculpture poodle.

What You'll Need

- heavy paper, such as drawing paper or construction paper
- craft knife or single-edged razor blade
- rubber cement or glue
- newspapers or thick cardboard
- notebook paper or typing paper
- ruler
- pencil
- scissors

Directions

1. Start with a sheet of heavy paper that is at least 12" x 8". Lay the paper horizontally. Put a stack of newspapers or a piece of thick cardboard underneath to protect your work surface.

2. With the pencil, draw a side view of a dog. You only need to draw one front leg and one back leg, but make them wide, because you will be scoring and bending them to look like four legs (A). Try to use up most of the paper. Then cut out the dog.

3. To score his legs, lightly draw a slightly curved line to divide the front leg into two legs. Do the same to the back leg. Then carefully run, or score, the back of the hobby knife or razor blade along the lines you drew (B). Press just hard enough to score the top layer of the paper. Don't cut right through the paper.

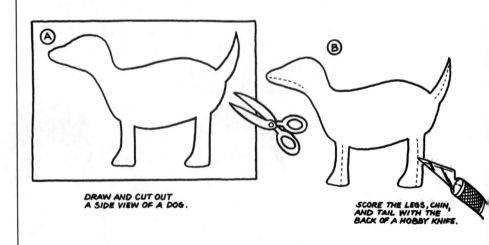

DRAW AND CUT OUT A SIDE VIEW OF A DOG.

SCORE THE LEGS, CHIN, AND TAIL WITH THE BACK OF A HOBBY KNIFE.

64

4. Now gently fold the legs along the cuts you made so that the lines you scored stick up and are outside the fold, facing you (C). Score the tail and chin the same way.

5. Next, you'll need to make fringes for your poodle's head, body, legs, and tail. Cut several strips of the notebook paper or typing paper. Each strip should be at least 2" wide. Vary the length depending on the size of the head, the tail, and so forth. Cut slits in each strip, then curl them by running them over the sharp edge of a scissors blade or a ruler (D).

6. Now attach each fringe of curls to your poodle using rubber cement or glue. Put each fringe right up against the other to create rows of curls. You can mount your paper sculpture by rubber-cementing it to a construction paper background of a contrasting color to make your art stand out (E).

One Step Further

You can create all sorts of things with paper sculpture—just put your mind to it! Use different-colored paper for variety. Cut semicircles and bend them out to make eyes, mouths, and other features. Once you know how to score the paper, you can create all sorts of three-dimensional effects. Just remember that the scored lines are always on the outside of the folds, so try scoring both sides of the paper and bending it both ways for that "3-D" look!

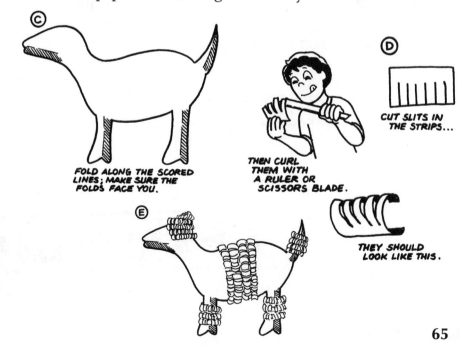

© FOLD ALONG THE SCORED LINES; MAKE SURE THE FOLDS FACE YOU.

THEN CURL THEM WITH A RULER OR SCISSORS BLADE.

Ⓓ CUT SLITS IN THE STRIPS...

THEY SHOULD LOOK LIKE THIS.

44 Magic Crystals

Use ordinary charcoal to grow colorful crystals right before your eyes!

What You'll Need

- charcoal briquettes
- disposable shallow cooking pan
- food coloring, any color
- paper cup
- mixing spoon
- 3 tablespoons salt
- 3 tablespoons liquid bluing (available at grocery stores)
- 3 tablespoons clear ammonia

Directions

1. Begin by spreading out enough charcoal briquettes to cover the bottom of the cooking pan.
2. Put a few drops of food coloring over the briquettes.
3. Mix the salt, bluing, and ammonia together in the paper cup and pour the solution over the charcoal. Be careful not to smell the ammonia directly. In just a few hours, crystals will start to grow!
4. You need to coat the charcoal with the solution each day. Just repeat Step 3. When you think they've grown enough, stop applying the liquid.

One Step Further

Try using different colors of food coloring to create two-tone or three-tone crystals. See if you can make the crystals grow into various shapes by pouring the ammonia solution over certain areas to create a pattern.

ADD A FEW DROPS OF FOOD COLORING.

THEN ADD THE AMMONIA MIXTURE.

45 **Bull-Roarer**

ADULT SUPERVISION REQUIRED

According to folklore, when the Native Americans whirled bull-roarers over their heads, the whooshing sound resembled the wind blowing. The Native Americans used bull-roarers to summon rain.

What You'll Need

- thin, flat piece of wood at least 6" long
- ruler
- sandpaper or a heavy file
- cord or string
- drill
- scissors

Directions

1. Get an adult to help you make the bull-roarer. The piece of wood can be any rectangular or square shape, just as long as it's thin and flat. Taper two opposing sides using the file or sandpaper. Then file down one end to create a rounded shape. File it down until it's smooth.

2. Next, drill a hole in the opposite end near the edge. Cut a piece of cord or string, 3' to 4' long. Put one end through the hole and tie a tight knot.

3. Now test your bull-roarer! It's best not to do this in the house. Go outside and stand in an area where you won't hit anything or anyone. Whirl the bull-roarer over your head in a fast circular motion. Don't be surprised if the sound comes and goes; that's how the bull-roarer works.

One Step Further

You can paint bright colors and patterns on your bull-roarer. Try making a bull-roarer using an oval or circular piece of wood this time. Try different sizes of wood, too. See if there's any difference in the sound each one makes.

WHIRRRRR!

FILE DOWN SIDES AND ROUND OFF THE TOP.

I Spy Tie-Dye

ADULT SUPERVISION REQUIRED

The art of tie-dyeing is so simple and fun, no wonder it's still as popular today as it was during the sixties!

What You'll Need

- empty 1-gallon bottle
- old clothes, such as T-shirts or shorts
- 3 plastic buckets or large bowls
- rubber gloves or clothespin
- bleach
- apron or smock
- string or rubber bands
- newspaper
- dye (Rit® or Tintex®), various colors
- old towels
- water

Directions

1. For light-colored fabric, use dye. For dark-colored fabric, use bleach. Put on the apron or smock before you start. To prepare the dye: Pour a package of dye powder, any color, into the gallon bottle and fill it with hot tap water. Put the top on and shake well. Pour the liquid into a plastic bucket or bowl. To prepare the bleach: Pour the bleach about 2" deep into another plastic bucket or bowl. Do this outside or near an open window. Don't touch the bleach or smell it directly! Fill the third bucket or bowl with plain water.

2. Now tie string or rubber bands around the fabric in as many places as you want (A).

TIE STRING OR RUBBER BANDS AROUND FABRIC. (A)

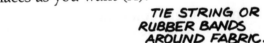

3. It is best to always wear rubber gloves when you're dipping fabric. If you don't have gloves, use a clothespin to pick up the fabric. Dip the fabric into the dye or bleach for two to three minutes (B). You can put the whole piece of fabric in, or just dip the parts that are tied. For light-colored fabrics, wait until the fabric is a little darker than you want it to be. For dark-colored fabrics, wait until it has turned as light as you want it to be.

4. Pick up the fabric and dip it into the bucket or bowl of plain water, then remove it and let it drip.

5. Wrap the fabric in some old towels and press down on it to soak up the water.

6. Take off the string or rubber bands and hang up the fabric to dry. Put newspapers below to catch any dripping water. You'll have a great piece of tie-dye overnight!

One Step Further

You can tie-dye the same shirt or piece of clothing in different colors. Get an extra bucket or bowl for each color. After the first dipping, rinse the fabric but don't remove the string or rubber bands. Then dip the fabric into a different-colored dye. Change the rinse water after each color. Try tie-dyeing old pillowcases or bedsheets!

Ⓑ USE A RUBBER GLOVE OR CLOTHES-PIN TO PICK UP FABRIC.

DIP FABRIC IN DYE OR BLEACH.

Dancing Marionettes

Everybody loves puppets. Here's how to make your very own marionette!

What You'll Need

- lightweight card-board, 8½" x 11"
- yarn, any color
- tempera paints or markers (various colors)
- 12" wooden stick
- scissors
- brass fasteners or rivets
- paintbrush
- hole punch
- heavy thread
- pencil
- glue
- ruler

Directions

1. Start by using the pencil to draw a person on the cardboard. Make sure the arms and legs are wide enough. Use the paint or markers to fill in the face and clothing.

2. Now cut the person out of the cardboard. To make hair, cut some short strands of yarn and glue them on top of the head.

3. Get ready to perform "surgery"! Cut off the feet, then cut again at the knees, then cut the legs off at the hips. Now cut off the hands, then cut at the elbows, then cut the arms off at the shoulders. All that's left should be the head and torso.

4. Next, punch holes in the arms and legs with the hole punch and use the brass fasteners to reattach each limb (A).

5. Now make the marionette's strings. Cut six 4" pieces of thread. Then cut six 9" pieces of thread. Tie the ends of the 4" pieces to the fasteners at the back of your marionette's wrists, elbows, and shoulders. Next, tie the longer pieces to the fasteners at the hips, knees, and feet.

6. One by one, tie the free ends to the wooden stick, spreading them out across the stick. The threads on the marionette's right side should be on the right half of the stick, and the threads on the puppet's left side should be on the left half. Rock the stick back and forth and watch your merry marionette dance (B)!

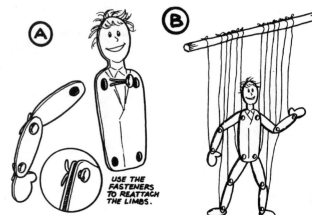

Ⓐ Ⓑ

USE THE FASTENERS TO REATTACH THE LIMBS.

Lionhearted!

Instead of throwing out old washcloths, save them to make a little washcloth lion face!

What You'll Need

- 2 old washcloths
- fabric scraps, old socks, yarn, foam rubber, cotton balls
- tape from an old audiocassette
- sewing machine (or needle and thread)
- buttons
- scissors
- felt
- fabric glue (available at craft stores)
- ruler

Directions

1. Start by making the lion's face on one of the washcloths. Sew on buttons for the lion's eyes. Cut pieces of felt for the ears, nose, whiskers, and mouth and glue them on.

2. To make the lion's mane, pull out the tape from an audiocassette. Cut the tape into 4"-long strips. Then lay down the second washcloth and glue the strips along the four sides of it so that they hang out over the sides (A). Overlap some of them to add thickness to the mane.

3. After the glue has dried, put any combination of fabric scraps, cutup socks, yarn, pieces of foam rubber, and cotton balls on top of the second washcloth. A handful or two should be enough.

4. Now place the first washcloth over the second one to cover the stuffing. Sew the washcloths together along all four sides, using small, tight stitches (A).

One Step Further

Try making a girl's or boy's face. Add human facial features using felt and buttons. Use cassette tape or colored yarn on the top side for hair.

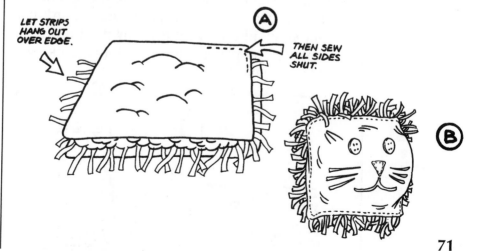

LET STRIPS HANG OUT OVER EDGE.

(A) THEN SEW ALL SIDES SHUT.

(B)

A Dandy Desk Set

If this "leather" desk set were real, it would probably cost $200, but you can make it for just pennies!

What You'll Need

- small glass bottle
- empty frozen juice can
- 12" x 18" piece of cardboard
- cigar box
- two 12" x 18" pieces of construction paper, any color
- empty baby food jar
- masking tape
- brown shoe polish
- newspaper
- ruler
- glue

Directions

1. First, lay down sheets of newspaper to cover your work surface. Clean and dry the frozen juice can. Tear off pieces of masking tape to cover the outside of the can completely.

2. Now rub shoe polish over the tape until all the pieces are colored brown. Once the polish is dry, you've got a pencil holder!

3. Repeat Steps 1 and 2, this time turning the baby food jar into a paper clip holder! Next, make the glass bottle into a flower vase or a letter-opener holder. Cover a cigar box with tape and polish and use it as a letter holder.

4. Now it's time to create a desk blotter. Take a sheet of the construction paper and cut out four right triangles with 3" bases (A). These will be the four corners of the blotter.

5. Cover the triangles with short strips of masking tape, then rub shoe polish over them. Lay a triangle on each corner of the piece of cardboard so that the right angles line up.

6. Next, carefully glue only the right edges of the triangles onto the cardboard. The edges that face toward the middle of the blotter should not be glued down. Insert the second piece of construction paper into your blotter, tucking a corner under each triangle (B).

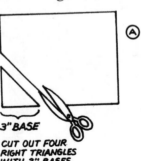

Ⓐ

3" BASE

CUT OUT FOUR RIGHT TRIANGLES WITH 3" BASES.

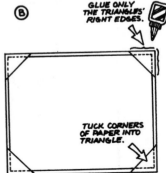

Ⓑ

GLUE ONLY THE TRIANGLES' RIGHT EDGES.

TUCK CORNERS OF PAPER INTO TRIANGLE.

Walking on Eggshells

Did you know you can dress up bottles, boxes, and cans with crushed eggshells? It's eggs-traordinary!

What You'll Need

- 12 raw eggs
- large mixing bowl
- glass bottle, shoe box, or tin can
- needle
- newspaper
- tempera paints, various colors
- glue
- paintbrush

Directions

1. Blow out the insides of the eggs first. Hold an egg over the mixing bowl. Make a hole in one end of the egg with the needle. Then make a hole in the other end, but don't take the needle out. Move the needle around inside the egg until the hole is about ½" wide. Remove the needle. Blow through the smaller hole. The inside of the egg will come out of the bigger hole. Rinse out the egg with cool water and repeat with the remaining eggs. (Don't throw the insides away—cook them for breakfast!)

2. Spread out a few sheets of newspaper and put the empty shells on top. Cover them with another sheet of newspaper. Now get your shoes on and stomp all over the shells to crush them. When you're through, take off the top sheet of newspaper.

3. Put glue all over the bottle, shoe box, or can. Then roll it in the crushed eggshells, making sure it gets completely covered. Let the glue dry.

4. Finally, use the tempera paints to paint the eggshells. Make stripes, polka dots, zigzag patterns . . . use your imagination!

Hosting a Craft Fair

Is everyone raving about the crafts you're making? Are you having so much fun that you don't want to stop? Well, have you ever thought about hosting a craft fair?

A craft fair is a great way to make some money. You can do it as a fund-raiser for a local charity or to get money for a neighborhood project. You can organize a craft fair to raise money for your school's student council. You can even hold a craft fair to make some money to buy a new bicycle.

Hosting a craft fair should be fun, but it requires a bit of thought and energy. Are you ready for a challenge? If you are, you can start preparing right now!

Four to eight weeks before the craft fair

The very first step is to get your parents' permission to host a craft fair. Assure them that you will be responsible for planning the whole event. You may have to borrow supplies or ask for assistance on occasion. It's a good idea to have an adult nearby during your craft fair in case you run into any problems.

Next, consider asking some friends to join you in hosting the craft fair. Invite friends who are responsible and reliable and, most importantly, will also enjoy making crafts. It will be easier and more fun to make crafts, distribute flyers, and organize the craft fair if you are working with friends. If you decide to host a craft fair on your own, try to keep it small. You don't need to do too much—a few nice crafts might be enough.

If you would like to hold a craft fair for a particular cause, present your idea to the other people involved. Prepare as much as possible beforehand so that you'll be ready to answer questions. Offer some ideas for crafts you can sell. Try to figure out how much work this craft fair will entail. Explain why a craft fair would be a great way to raise money for the cause. Be sure to encourage others to share their ideas for the craft fair.

There are many different crafts in this book that you could make for your craft fair. Keep in mind which ones will be easiest to make and which ones might sell well. See pages 78–79 for some ideas. Once you decide which crafts to sell, figure out how many of each craft you will need to make. For example, you could make about six mini-piñatas, rather than one big piñata. Start making crafts as soon as you've set your list. Store them in a safe spot until the craft fair.

Do you want to have a theme for your craft fair? You can try a summer theme or a holiday theme. You can also give your craft fair a creative name to make it more fun. Brainstorm with your friends or look through magazines and newspapers for interesting names or themes.

Choose the location for your craft fair. If you're raising money for a particular cause, you may be able to have the sale at school. Ask a teacher to help you find out what the rules are. If not, choose someone's home. Have it outside (as long as the weather is nice) if you want to catch customers who are just driving by. Ask an adult to check on any neighborhood or city regulations against holding a yard sale. If you are having it inside, consider making the craft fair invitation-only so it's not too crowded.

Decide on a date for your craft fair. It's important to consider how long it will take you to make all the crafts you want to sell. Give yourself plenty of time to work on them after school and on the weekends. When you've come up with a reasonable amount of time, tack on an extra week just in case you run into problems. Ask adults who will be involved what time will be convenient for them. Make sure you select a time when your customers will be able to come. If you're having your craft fair at home, a Saturday or Sunday might be most convenient. If you're selling crafts at school, after the last class or during lunchtime may work the best.

Pick a starting time and an ending time. Make sure you allow yourself plenty of time to set everything up and clean up afterward. A few hours should be plenty of time for your craft fair, unless you have a lot of people who can take turns selling. You'll need to schedule in breaks if you're selling all day!

Two to three weeks before the craft fair

Now invite your friends and family. You can make invitations if you're only giving them to a few people. If you want to attract a lot of customers, you can make flyers and hand them out to people in your community. The invitations or flyers should include the following information:

- who is hosting the craft fair
- what you will be selling—list a few of your favorite crafts
- when it will be—what time it will begin and end, and the date
- where it will be—include directions if necessary
- why you're hosting the craft fair—but only if it's for a cause you think people would be interested in

If you have decided on an invitation-only craft fair, you might want to ask people to RSVP. Include your name and phone number on the invitations so that it will be easy for them to contact you. If you are passing out flyers, make sure that you get a parent's permission first. *Do not put your phone number on flyers that you will be handing out to strangers.*

If your craft fair has a theme or a unique name, be sure to include this on the invitations or flyers. Try to make them fun and creative! Think about how many you will need to make. If it's a lot, consider photocopying them, but plan carefully so that you don't waste money.

As the date of the craft fair nears, keep making crafts. If you're running into problems with any of the crafts, you still have time to choose new ones.

The week before the craft fair

Are all the crafts ready? Add any finishing touches and check over your work.

A few days before the craft fair, decide how much to charge for each craft. Keep track of how much each item cost to make, then add on a bit, or double the amount, to get the price. When you've done that, ask yourself if people will be willing to pay that much. For example, figure out how much it will cost you to make "Works Like a Charm!" on page 13. Is $1.00 too much to charge for it? You and the other craft fair organizers should also decide ahead of time whether or not you will be willing to accept bargaining. A customer may offer to pay you less than what's on the price tag. Will you accept that?

Mark each item's price on a tag. You can use removable stickers, index cards, or signs to display the prices. Make sure the price tags don't damage the crafts. Write the price clearly.

You will need a cash box and some money to make change for your customers. If you don't have a cash box, you can use a shoe box. A calculator may also come in handy. Be sure that you have a pad of paper and a few pencils. Write down each craft item and its price when you sell it. This will help you keep track of which items are selling quickly and how much they have sold for, so that you'll have an idea of what to make for your next craft fair.

Now think of what other materials you will need for the day of the fair. You may need to buy some items. These items cut into your profits, so try to borrow them whenever possible. Ask your parents to save paper bags and boxes for you to use. Try to arrange the crafts on tables with tablecloths if possible. If you don't have tables, you can turn over boxes, cover them with fabric, and place the crafts on top. Presentation is very important, so try to make things look nice.

Give yourself enough time to set everything up before the craft fair begins. Take some time to decorate the area. You can tie a few balloons to the tables or arrange some artificial flowers. Do you have a theme that would be fun to decorate with? Put up signs to grab people's attention, but make sure you have permission first.

The day of the craft fair

Concentrate on having fun! All the hard work you did ahead of time should pay off. Be friendly to your customers. Make yourself available to answer questions.

When it's all done, don't forget to clean up thoroughly, and thank everyone who has helped you.

Whether you're having your craft fair after school or on the weekend, you can bet that you'll work up an appetite! Keep some fruit and crackers on hand for a snack. Or if you think you'll be really hungry, pack a cooler with sandwiches. Also, be sure to have a supply of water nearby.

The Perfect Craft

Although you should be able to make the crafts in this book using items normally found around your home, you may want to buy some materials. If you decide to do that, keep in mind that it will cut into your profits. There are many ways to make the crafts especially appealing—here are a few items that could be best-sellers at a craft fair.

It's a Piñata! (page 19)

Create a bunch of mini-piñatas using small balloons. Sell them with wrapped candies and small toys stuffed inside. With this item, it's a good idea to keep track of what's inside each piñata so that customers can know what they're buying.

Marvelous Marbleized Stationery (page 20)

Create a pencil and paper set your customers will love! Follow the steps described for the craft to make a matching pencil. Attach a clothespin to the eraser, then dip a pencil in the oil paint. Stick the sharpened end of the pencil into a piece of Styrofoam to keep it steady and let it dry overnight.

Candle, Candle, Burning Bright (page 34)

When you're ready to pour the wax into the cartons, ask an adult to carefully drop in rose petals, leaves, and small twigs, or line the milk or juice cartons with these items before you pour in the wax. When the candle is set, wrap a pretty ribbon around the middle of the candle and tie it into a bow.

Paper Perfect (page 48)

Add dried flower petals, leaves, and tiny twigs to the pulp to make some really pretty paper. When the paper is ready, you can stack a few sheets together, tie a ribbon around them, and add a dried flower to finish off the set.

I Spy Tie-Dye (page 68)

Create cool T-shirt and sock sets, or make tie-dyed hair bands. Find clothing items that are made of cotton and are white and washable. Follow the directions with this craft to make different pieces.

Does your craft fair have a theme? If it does, then select some crafts that could follow the theme. Try to think of simple ways you could adapt them. Here's how to make a few crafts for a beach-theme craft fair.

Works Like a Charm! (page 13)

Spread glue over the wooden frame, then cover it with shells and sprinkle on colored sand. After it dries, take it outside, place it on newspaper, and spray it with shellac.

Sublime Chimes (page 14)

This craft would look great with a beach theme! Glue rope around the edges of the cardboard. Cover the cardboard and rope with gold spray paint. After it dries, glue some seashells to the cardboard. Then place additional seashells on string (or glue them to the string) and hang them from the cardboard to catch the wind.

Soapy Sculptures (page 53)

Shape soap into seashells, starfish, or sea lions. You can create a number of fun beach or sea items.

Did your little brother help you set up tables? Did your mom save the day when it started to rain? When the craft fair is over and you've cleaned everything up, there's only one thing left to do. It's time to say thank you to everyone who has helped you out. Make each person's gift unique. With a little extra thought, a set of "Rolling Coasters" or "Sublime Chimes" can make a wonderful gift. If you can, make your thank-you gifts before the craft fair. Otherwise, make them as soon as possible. You should give the gifts to everyone within one week of the craft fair.

Craft Fair Checkoff List

Create your own checkoff list with all the things you'll need to keep track of for your craft fair. You can do it on a computer or by hand. Be sure to include all the important information, as shown on the example below. You can also include flyers/invitations, price tags, signs, and thank-you gifts on your list.

Specifics

Theme: _____

Date: _____

Time: _____ to _____

Place: _____

Other crafters   Phone numbers

_____   _____

_____   _____

_____   _____

Decorations

Need to make   Need to buy

_____   _____

_____   _____

_____   _____

Supplies

Supplies	Number	Who will bring it/buy it
Tables	_____	_____
Chairs	_____	_____
Pencils	_____	_____
Pads of paper	_____	_____
Calculator	_____	_____
Cash box	_____	_____
_____	_____	_____
_____	_____	_____
_____	_____	_____
_____	_____	_____

Crafts

Craft: _____ Done _____

Number	Materials	Who will bring it/buy it
_____	_____	_____
_____	_____	_____
_____	_____	_____